MW01118114

THE
CONSTITUTION

History SparkNotes

Spark Educational Publishing
A Division of Barnes & Noble Publishing
120 Fifth Avenue
New York, NY 10011
www.sparknotes.com

ISBN 1-4114-0418-1

Please submit all comments and questions or report errors to *www.sparknotes.com/errors*.

Printed and bound in the United States.

CONTENTS

OVERVIEW

A fter their victory in the American Revolution, America's leaders were leery about establishing a powerful central-ized government, fearful that such a government would only replace the tyranny of King George III with a new form of tyranny. As a result, the first U.S. constitution, the Articles of Confederation, created a decentralized new government. The Articles established the United States as a confederation of states—a system in which the states were largely independent but were bound together by a weak national congress.

Ultimately, the Articles of Confederation proved ineffective, giv-ing Congress little real power over the states, no means to enforce its decisions, and, most critically, no power to levy taxes. As a result, the federal government was left at the mercy of the states, which often chose not to pay their taxes.

Sensing the need for change, delegates from nearly all the states met in 1787 to revise the Articles of Confederation but ended up drafting an entirely new document: the Constitution. The Constitu-tion created a new government divided into three branches: legisla-tive (Congress), executive (the president), and judicial (headed by the Supreme Court). After much debate, the delegates compromised on a two-house Congress, consisting of an upper house (Senate) with equal representation for each state, and a lower house (House of Representatives) with proportional representation based on pop-ulation. Congress also was given new abilities to levy national taxes and control interstate commerce.

Although most states ratified the Constitution outright, some, especially New York, had reservations. In response, Alexander Hamilton, John Jay, and James Madison argued the case for the Constitution in a series of essays called the Federalist Papers. These eighty-five essays are now regarded as some of the most important writings in American political thought.

However, many skeptics, or Anti-Federalists, remained uncon-vinced, believing that a stronger government would endanger the freedoms they had just won during the Revolution. As a compro-mise, the framers of the Constitution promised to add a series of amendments to guarantee important liberties. Sponsored by James Madison, the first ten amendments became known as the Bill of

Rights. Their liberties secured, Anti-Federalists in the last remaining states grudgingly voted for the Constitution.

The 1790s were rocky for the United States: the new government functioned well, but disputes arose about how the government should act in situations in which the Constitution was vague. The foremost of these disagreements involved the question of whether or not the federal government had the right to found a national bank. "Strict constructionists" such as Thomas Jefferson interpreted the Constitution literally, believing that the document forbade everything it did not expressly permit. "Loose constructionists" such as Alexander Hamilton believed that the Constitution's "elastic clause" permitted everything the document did not expressly forbid—such as the founding of a bank.

Hamilton and Jefferson disagreed often during George Washington's presidency, and eventually their ideas spread through the country and coalesced into the nation's first two political parties, the Hamiltonian Federalists and the Jeffersonian Democratic-Republicans. Although Washington begged Americans not to separate into dangerous political factions—for he believed that factions and political parties would destroy the republican spirit and tear the Union apart—the party system developed. Indeed, Washington's successor, the Federalist John Adams, tried to ruin the opposition party with his 1798 Sedition Act, which ultimately only made the Democratic-Republicans stronger.

When Adams's bitter rival Jefferson was elected president in 1800, many European observers thought the American "experiment" in republicanism would end. But when the transfer of power proved to be peaceful, many Europeans, seeing that republicanism could be viable and stable, began to believe the system might work for them too. The U.S. triumph over Britain and success in establishing a stable government had already encouraged the French to overthrow their own monarch in the French Revolution of 1789. Later, republicanism and democracy would spread beyond France to Britain and the rest of Europe. Thus, the drafting of the Constitution and the years that followed were enormously important in world history as well as American history.

Summary of Events

The Articles of Confederation
After declaring independence from Britain in 1776, the delegates at the **Second Continental Congress** immediately set to the task of creating a government. In 1777, Congress submitted the nation's first constitution, the **Articles of Confederation**, to the states, who finally ratified it a few years later.

Problems Under the Articles
Congress proved unable to manage the country's economic affairs under the Articles. Because most state currencies had become useless due to wartime **inflation**, Congress printed its own continental dollars to keep the economy alive, but these faltered as well. Congress also proved unable to raise enough money from the states, because the federal government had no way of forcing the states to pay taxes. Most states also ignored Congress's attempts to resolve numerous interstate disputes that arose.

In addition, many Americans became fed up with their incompetent state legislatures and demanded debt relief and cheaper money. A few even revolted, as in **Shays's Rebellion** in 1786–1787, which culminated in Daniel Shays leading 1,200 western Massachusetts farmers in an attack on the federal arsenal at Springfield. Although the rebellion was quickly dismissed, it convinced many American leaders that change was needed if the U.S. were to survive.

Drafting the Constitution
To resolve these problems, delegates from most of the states met at the **Annapolis Convention** in 1786. When nothing was resolved, they agreed to reconvene in 1787 at a **Constitutional Convention** in Philadelphia. At this second convention, it was quickly decided that an entirely new constitution was needed rather than just a revision to the Articles.

A major point of contention was the structure of the new **legislative** branch. Small states supported the **New Jersey Plan**, under which all states would have equal representation in the legislature. Large states advocated the **Virginia Plan** to create a bicameral (two-house) legislature in which representatives would be appointed according to population. The **Great Compromise** among the states created a bicameral Congress in which states would be equally represented in the **Senate** and proportionally represented in the **House of Representatives**.

The framers of the Constitution believed strongly in **checks and balances** and **separation of powers** to prevent any one branch of government from ever becoming too powerful. As a result, the new government would also have a strong **executive** branch and an independent **judiciary** branch.

THE FEDERALIST PAPERS AND THE
BILL OF RIGHTS

When the delegates submitted the Constitution to the states for ratification, heated debates erupted between the **Federalists**, who supported the Constitution, and the **Anti-Federalists**, who thought it gave the federal government too much power. Federalists **Alexander Hamilton, John Jay,** and **James Madison** coauthored the **Federalist Papers** in 1787–1788 to convince Anti-Federalist Americans, especially in New York, that the Constitution was necessary. Eventually, the Anti-Federalists conceded on the condition that a **Bill of Rights** be written to preserve liberties, such as freedoms of speech and religion and the right to trial by jury.

STRICT VS. LOOSE CONSTRUCTIONISM

The Electoral College unanimously chose **George Washington** to be the first president, with **John Adams** as vice president. Soon after, the new secretary of the treasury, **Alexander Hamilton**, wanted to repair the national credit and revive the economy by having the federal government assume all the debts of the individual states. He also wanted to establish a national **Bank of the United States**. The Constitution said nothing about a national bank, but Hamilton believed that the Constitution allowed many unwritten actions that it did not expressly forbid. **Thomas Jefferson**, the secretary of state and a **strict constructionist**, believed that the Constitution forbade everything it did not allow. These ideological differences within Washington's cabinet formed the basis of what later became full-fledged political parties—the Hamiltonian Federalists and the Jeffersonian **Democratic-Republicans**.

DOMESTIC UNREST IN THE 1790S

Despite the passage of the **Indian Intercourse Acts**, beginning in 1790, Native Americans frequently raided American settlements west of the Appalachians until federal troops crushed several tribes in the **Battle of Fallen Timbers** in 1794.

Later, when farmers in western Pennsylvania threatened to march on Philadelphia to protest the **excise tax** on liquor in 1794, Washington dispatched 13,000 federal troops to crush the insurgents. The **Whiskey Rebellion**, however, ended without bloodshed.

WASHINGTON AND NEUTRALITY

Events in Europe also affected the United States. The **French Revolution** of 1789 and France's subsequent war with Britain split American public opinion: some wanted to support republican France, while others wanted to help England. However, under the Franco-American alliance of 1778, the United States was obligated to assist France.

Unprepared for another war, Washington issued the **Neutrality Proclamation of 1793**. Citizen Genêt, the French ambassador to the United States, ignored the proclamation and, immediately upon his arrival in the United States, began commissioning privateers and planning to use U.S. ports in the French campaign against Britain. Outraged over the **Citizen Genêt affair**, Washington requested Genet's recall.

Meanwhile, Spain threatened to block Americans' access to the vital Mississippi River, while Britain still refused to withdraw from American territory in the Ohio Valley. These issues were not resolved until **Jay's Treaty** with Britain in 1794 and **Pinckney's Treaty** in 1795.

Finally, in his famous **Farewell Address** in 1796, Washington warned against entangling alliances with European powers and potential political factions in the United States.

ADAMS'S TERM

In 1797, Washington was succeeded by his Federalist vice president, **John Adams**, who faced continued challenges from Europe. When Adams sent an ambassador to Paris to restore Franco-American relations, three French officials demanded a bribe before they would speak with him. This incident, the **XYZ Affair**, shocked Americans and initiated two years of undeclared naval warfare.

To prevent unwanted French immigrants from entering the country, Adams and a sympathetic Congress passed the **Alien Acts** in 1798. They also passed the **Sedition Act**, which banned public criticism of the government in an attempt to stifle political opposition and wipe out the Democratic-Republicans. Thomas Jefferson and James Madison responded with the **Virginia and Kentucky Resolutions**, which nullified the Sedition Act in those states. They argued that because the states had created the Union, they also had the right to nullify any unconstitutional legislation.

THE ELECTION OF 1800

The Democratic-Republicans defeated the Federalists in the election of 1800. Despite years of mutual hatred, the Federalists relinquished the government to their political enemies in a peaceful transfer of power. **Thomas Jefferson**, champion of western and southern farmers, became president and immediately advocated a reduction in the size and power of the federal government.

INCREASES IN FEDERAL POWER

In reality, federal power *increased* in many ways during Jefferson's eight years in office. The Supreme Court reasserted its power of judicial review in the 1803 *Marbury v. Madison* decision. Jefferson's **Louisiana Purchase** more than doubled the size of the country despite the fact that the Constitution said nothing about new land purchases.

THE EMBARGO ACT

Jefferson continued to face challenges from Europe, as neither Britain nor France respected American **shipping rights** as a neutral country. Both countries seized hundreds of American merchant ships bound for Europe, and British warships **impressed** (captured for forced labor) thousands of American sailors. To end these practices, Jefferson and Congress passed the **Embargo Act** in 1807, closing all U.S. ports to export shipping and placing restrictions on imports from Britain. Unfortunately, the boycott backfired, and the U.S. economy slumped as Britain and France found other sources of natural resources.

THE NON-INTERCOURSE ACT AND
MACON'S BILL NO. 2

Congress repealed the **Embargo Act** in 1809 but replaced it with the **Non-Intercourse Act**, which banned trade only with Britain and France. A year later, with **James Madison** in office as president, the American economy still had not improved, so Congress passed **Macon's Bill No. 2**, which restored trade relations with all nations but promised to revive the Non-Intercourse Act if either Britain or France violated U.S. shipping rights.

THE WAR OF 1812

Meanwhile, **War Hawks** in Congress from the West and South pressed Madison for war against the British and **Tecumseh**'s Native

American **Northwest Confederacy**. Tecumseh's forces were defeated at the **Battle of Tippecanoe** in 1811. Since the British were still seizing American ships and impressing American sailors, Congress declared war on Britain in 1812.

The **War of 1812** was primarily a sectional conflict supported by Americans in the West and South and condemned by those in the Northeast. In 1814, delegates from the New England states met at the **Hartford Convention** to petition Congress and redress grievances. By the time Congress received their complaint, however, the war had ended and the **Treaty of Ghent** had been signed.

SUMMARY OF EVENTS

KEY PEOPLE & TERMS

PEOPLE

JOHN ADAMS
A prominent Boston lawyer who first became famous for defending the British soldiers accused of murdering five civilians in the **Boston Massacre**. At the **Continental Congresses**, Adams acted as a delegate from Massachusetts and rejected proposals for self-governance within the British Empire. He served as vice president to George Washington and then as president from 1797–1801.

SAMUEL ADAMS
A second cousin of John Adams and a failed Bostonian businessman who became an ardent political activist in the years leading up to the Revolutionary War. Samuel Adams organized the first **Committee of Correspondence** and was a delegate to both Continental Congresses in 1774 and 1775.

ALEXANDER HAMILTON
A brilliant New York lawyer and statesman who, in his early thirties, was one of the youngest delegates at the Constitutional Convention in 1787. An ardent **Federalist,** Hamilton supported the Constitution during the ratification debates even though he actually believed that the new document was still too weak. He helped write the **Federalist Papers**, which are now regarded as some of the finest essays on American government and republicanism. He served as the first secretary of the treasury under George Washington and established the first **Bank of the United States**.

WILLIAM HENRY HARRISON
A former governor of Indiana Territory and brigadier general in the U.S. Army who rose to national stardom when he defeated the Northwest Confederacy at the **Battle of Tippecanoe** in 1811. Harrison went on to be elected president in 1840.

PATRICK HENRY
A fiery radical who advocated **rebellion** against the Crown in the years prior to the American Revolution, as in his famous "Give me

liberty or give me death" speech. Later, Henry was a die-hard **Anti-Federalist** who initially opposed ratification of the Constitution.

ANDREW JACKSON
A hero of the **War of 1812** and the **Creek War** who later entered the national political arena and became president in 1829. Jackson, nicknamed "Old Hickory," was the first U.S. president to come from a region west of the Appalachians.

JOHN JAY
A coauthor of the **Federalist Papers**, which attempted to convince Anti-Federalist New Yorkers to ratify the Constitution. Jay served as the first Chief Justice of the Supreme Court and became one of the most hated men in America after he negotiated **Jay's Treaty** with Britain in 1794.

THOMAS JEFFERSON
A Virginia planter and lawyer who in 1776 drafted the **Declaration of Independence,** which justified American independence from Britain. Jefferson went on to serve as the first secretary of state under George Washington and as vice president under John Adams. He then was elected president himself in 1800 and 1804.

JAMES MADISON
A Virginia Federalist who advocated for the ratification of the Constitution, coauthored the **Federalist Papers**, and sponsored the **Bill of Rights** in Congress. After ratification, he supported southern and western agrarian interests as a **Democratic-Republican**. After a brief retirement, he reentered politics and was elected president in 1808 and 1812. As president, Madison fought for U.S. **shipping rights** against British and French aggression and led the country during the **War of 1812**.

JAMES MONROE
A Virginia officer, lawyer, and **Democratic-Republican** who was elected president in 1816 and inaugurated the Era of Good Feelings. An excellent administrator, Monroe bolstered the federal government and supported internal improvements, and was so popular in his first term that he ran uncontested in 1820. The "good feelings" ended, however, during the **Missouri Crisis** that split the United States along north-south lines. Monroe is most famous for his 1823 **Monroe Doctrine,** which warned European powers against interfering in the Western Hemisphere.

KEY PEOPLE & TERMS

TECUMSEH

A member of the Shawnee tribe who, along with his brother **Tensk-watawa** (often called the Prophet), organized many of the tribes in the Mississippi Valley into the **Northwest Confederacy** to defend Native American ancestral lands from white American settlers. Even though the tribes had legal rights to their lands under the **Indian Intercourse Acts** of the 1790s, expansionist War Hawks in Congress argued the need for action against Tecumseh, and eventually **William Henry Harrison** was sent to wipe out the Confederacy. Tecumseh's forces were defeated at the **Battle of Tippecanoe** in 1811.

GEORGE WASHINGTON

A Virginia planter and militia officer who led the attack that initiated the **French and Indian War** in 1754. Washington later became commander in chief of the American forces during the **American Revolution** and first president of the United States in 1789. Although he lost many of the military battles he fought, his leadership skills were unparalleled and were integral to the creation of the United States. In his noteworthy **Farewell Address**, Washington warned against factionalism and the formation of political parties, believing they would split the nation irreparably.

TERMS

ALIEN ACTS

A group of acts passed in 1798, designed to restrict the freedom of foreigners in the United States and curtail the free press in anticipation of a war with France. The Alien Acts lengthened the residency time required for foreigners to become American citizens from five years to fourteen years and gave the president the power to expel aliens considered dangerous to the nation. It was passed simultaneously with the **Sedition Act,** and together they provoked the **Virginia and Kentucky Resolutions,** written the same year in protest. These resolutions stated that individual states had the right to nullify unconstitutional laws passed by Congress.

ANNAPOLIS CONVENTION

A meeting of delegates from five states in Annapolis, Maryland, in 1786 to discuss the bleak commercial situation in the United States, growing social unrest, and Congress's inability to resolve disputes among the states. The conference dissolved when Alexander Hamil-

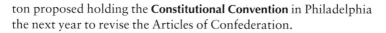

ton proposed holding the **Constitutional Convention** in Philadelphia the next year to revise the Articles of Confederation.

ANTI-FEDERALISTS

Primarily farmers and poorer Americans in the West, a group that strongly opposed ratification of the **Constitution**. The Anti-Federalists were suspicious of governments in general and a strong central government in particular. Rather, they believed that state legislatures should maintain sovereignty. Although they eventually lost the ratification battle, their protests did encourage the first Congress to attach the **Bill of Rights** to the Constitution.

ARTICLES OF CONFEDERATION

The first U.S. constitution, adopted in 1777 and ratified in 1781. The Articles established a national Congress in which each state in the Union was granted one vote. Congress had the right to conduct foreign affairs, maintain a military, govern western territories, and regulate trade between states, but it could not levy taxes. Because most states refused to finance the Congress adequately, the government under the Articles was doomed to fail. After **Shays's Rebellion** in 1786–1787, delegates met to discuss revising the Articles of Confederation, which ultimately led to the drafting of the **Constitution**.

BANK OF THE UNITED STATES

A plan proposed by **Alexander Hamilton** for a treasury for federal money funded by private investors. The Bank sparked a debate between **"strict constructionists"** and **"loose constructionists"** regarding interpretation of the Constitution.

BILL OF RIGHTS

The first ten amendments to the Constitution, sponsored in Congress by **James Madison**, to guarantee basic freedoms and liberties. The Bill of Rights protects freedoms of speech, press, religion, assembly, and petition, and the rights to have trial by jury, bear arms, and own property, among others. Moreover, the Ninth Amendment states that the people have additional rights beyond those written explicitly in the Constitution; the Tenth Amendment awards state governments all the powers not granted to the federal government. The promise of a Bill of Rights helped convince many **Anti-Federalists** to ratify the new Constitution. Today, these rights are considered fundamental American liberties.

CHECKS AND BALANCES
A term referring to the overlapping of powers granted to the three branches of government under the **Constitution**. For example, Congress has the power to pass laws and regulate taxes, but the president has the ability to veto, or nullify, those acts. On the other hand, Congress may override a president's veto if two-thirds of its members support the bill in question. The Supreme Court, meanwhile, has the power to review all laws but must rely on the president to enforce its decisions. The framers of the Constitution included this system of checks and balances to prevent any one branch of government from having too much power over the others.

CONSTITUTION
A 1787 document that established the structure of the U.S. government, drafted at the **Constitutional Convention** in Philadelphia by prominent statesmen from twelve states (minus Rhode Island). Unlike its predecessor, the **Articles of Confederation**, the Constitution established a strong central government divided into three separate but equal branches (legislative, executive, and judiciary). This **separation of powers**, combined with a system of **checks and balances**, was designed to prevent the new government from becoming too strong and tyrannical.

CONSTITUTIONAL CONVENTION
A 1787 meeting in Philadelphia in which delegates from twelve states convened to revise the **Articles of Confederation**. The Convention quickly decided that the Articles should be scrapped and replaced with an entirely new document to create a stronger central government binding the states. The result was the **Constitution**.

DECLARATION OF INDEPENDENCE
A document written by **Thomas Jefferson** in 1776 that proclaimed the creation of the United States. The Declaration sets forth a persuasive argument against King George III, claiming that the king ruled the colonies poorly and unjustly. The document thus served not merely as a declaration but also as a rational justification for breaking away from Britain.

DEMOCRATIC-REPUBLICANS
Successors of the **Anti-Federalists** who formed a party under **Thomas Jefferson**'s leadership during Washington's and Adams's presidencies. The Democratic-Republicans generally favored westward expansion, the formation of an agrarian republic, and an alliance

with France, and were **strict constructionists** and advocates of **states' rights.** Political battles between the Democratic-Republicans and the Federalists were frequent during the first years of the nineteenth century. Though the Federalist Party died out during the War of 1812, the Democratic-Republicans lived on during the Era of Good Feelings and eventually became the Democratic Party.

ELASTIC CLAUSE
A nickname for Article I, Section VIII, Paragraph 18 of the **Constitution,** which states that Congress has the power "to make all laws which shall be necessary and proper" to carry out its proscribed duties. **Alexander Hamilton** and the **Federalists** interpreted this clause to mean that the Constitution allows everything it does not expressly forbid, and used it to justify the creation of the **Bank of the United States. George Washington** agreed, and the clause has since given presidents and Congress ample justification for expanding federal power. The clause has been dubbed "elastic" because it gives federal policymakers great flexibility when drafting laws.

ELECTORAL COLLEGE
A body of representatives appointed by states to cast their votes for president. The presidential candidate who receives the most Electoral College votes, regardless of how many popular votes he or she receives, becomes president. The framers of the **Constitution** created the Electoral College out of fear that the whimsical American masses might one day popularly elect someone "unfit" for the presidency.

EXCISE TAX OF 1791
A liquor tax proposed by **Alexander Hamilton** in 1790 to raise revenue so that Congress could pay off all national and state debts. The excise tax was immensely unpopular with western farmers, whose protests eventually culminated in the **Whiskey Rebellion** of 1794.

THE FEDERALIST PAPERS
A series of eighty-five articles written by **James Madison, Alexander Hamilton,** and **John Jay** in 1787–1788 to convince New Yorkers to ratify the **Constitution.** The Federalist Papers are now regarded as some of the finest essays on the Constitution, American government, and republicanism.

FEDERALISTS
Primarily from the wealthier and propertied classes of Americans along the eastern seaboard, a group that supported ratification of

the **Constitution** and creation of a **strong central government**. The Federalists eventually became a full-fledged political party under the leadership of John Adams and Alexander Hamilton. Adams was the first and only Federalist president, as the party died after Federalist delegates from the **Hartford Convention** protested the War of 1812 and were labeled traitors.

GREAT COMPROMISE

An agreement between the large and small states at the **Constitutional Convention** of 1787 to create a **bicameral** (two-house) Congress with one chamber of delegates assigned based on population (the **House of Representatives**) and another chamber in which all states had two representatives regardless of population (the **Senate**). The agreement ended the deadlock among the states and set a precedent for compromise in American politics.

HARTFORD CONVENTION

An 1814–1815 meeting of delegates from five New England states in Hartford, Connecticut, to discuss possible secession from the Union due to discontent with the **War of 1812**. The delegates ultimately decided to remain in the Union but sent a petition to Congress, requesting amendments to the **Constitution** in order to alter the office of the presidency and to change the distribution and powers of Congress. None of their demands were met, however, because the petition arrived at Congress during celebrations over **Andrew Jackson**'s victory at the **Battle of New Orleans** and the signing of the **Treaty of Ghent**. Nonetheless, the convention demonstrated the sectional nature of the war and the growing differences between the North and the South.

INDIAN INTERCOURSE ACTS

A series of acts passed in the 1790s that attempted to smooth relations between the United States and Native American tribes along the western frontier. The act attempted to regulate trade between these groups and promised that the United States would acquire western lands only via treaties. Most American settlers ignored this bill, which produced bloody clashes between tribes and settlers.

JUDICIARY ACT OF 1789

The first act that Congress passed, which created the tiered U.S. federal court system. The Supreme Court, under Chief Justice **John Jay**, was at the head of the court system, supported by three circuit courts and thirteen district courts. Even though the Judiciary Act strengthened federal judicial power, it also upheld local and state courts by stipulating that most cases heard in federal courts would be appeals cases.

LAND ORDINANCE OF 1785
An ordinance passed by the national Congress under the **Articles of Confederation** that established an efficient system to survey and auction lands west of the Appalachian Mountains.

LOOSE CONSTRUCTIONISTS
People such as **Alexander Hamilton**, who believed that the **Constitution** allowed the government to take any actions that were not expressly forbidden in the document. The loose constructionists' interpretation was challenged by Thomas Jefferson and other **strict constructionists**, who believed that the Constitution must be read literally.

MACON'S BILL NO. 2
An 1810 bill that restored U.S. commerce with Britain and France (after their interruption under the **Embargo Act** and **Non-Intercourse Act**) but threatened to revive the terms of the Non-Intercourse Act if either country failed to respect U.S. neutrality and shipping rights.

NEW JERSEY PLAN
Also known as the **small state plan**, a proposal at the 1787 Constitutional Convention to create a **unicameral** (single-house) legislature in which all states would be equally represented. The New Jersey plan appealed to smaller states but not to more populous states, which backed the **Virginia Plan** to create a bicameral legislature in which representatives were apportioned by population. The **Great Compromise** solved the dilemma by creating a bicameral Congress featuring one house with proportional representation and another with equal representation.

NON-INTERCOURSE ACT
An 1809 act that replaced the ineffective **Embargo Act** in an attempt to revive the faltering American economy by boosting U.S. exports. The Non-Intercourse Act banned trade only with France and Britain (unlike the Embargo Act, which banned exports completely) until both nations agreed to respect American sovereignty. When this bill also failed, Congress passed **Macon's Bill No. 2**.

NORTHWEST CONFEDERACY
A confederation of Native American tribes in the Mississippi Valley, led by Tecumseh and his brother, for mutual defense against white

settlers. Although the tribes of the Northwest Confederacy had legal rights to their lands under the **Indian Intercourse Acts** of the 1790s, expansionist War Hawks in Congress nonetheless prevailed, and **William Henry Harrison** was sent to wipe out the Confederacy. Tecumseh's forces were defeated at the **Battle of Tippecanoe** in 1811.

NORTHWEST ORDINANCE OF 1787

A framework passed by the national Congress under the **Articles of Confederation** to decide which western U.S. territories (Ohio, Michigan, Wisconsin, Illinois, and Indiana) could become states. Because the ordinance also abolished slavery and established basic civil liberties (trial by jury, freedom of religion) in the Northwest Territory, it is often seen as an important first step toward the creation of the **Bill of Rights**.

SECOND CONTINENTAL CONGRESS

A meeting of colonial delegates that convened in different places from 1775 to 1789 to establish a new U.S. government after declaring independence from Britain. In 1777, the Congress drafted the **Articles of Confederation** as the first U.S. constitution.

SEDITION ACT

A 1798 act (passed simultaneously with the **Alien Acts**) that banned all forms of public expression critical of the president or Congress. President John Adams approved the act, fearing the influence of French immigrants in the United States and also hoping the free speech ban would harm his political opponents, the **Democratic-Republicans**. Ironically, the act only made the opposition party stronger. Thomas Jefferson and James Madison wrote the **Virginia and Kentucky Resolutions** the same year in protest, arguing that individual states had the right to nullify unconstitutional laws passed by Congress.

SEPARATION OF POWERS

A term referring to the fact that each of the three branches in the American federal government has separate and distinct powers. The **legislative** branch, for example, has the sole ability to propose and pass laws, while the **executive** branch has the power to enforce those laws, and the **judiciary** the power to review them. The writers of the Constitution separated these powers to prevent any one part of the new government from becoming too powerful.

Shays's Rebellion

A 1786–1787 revolt by western Massachusetts farmer **Daniel Shays**, who led 1,200 other men in an attack on the federal arsenal at Springfield, Massachusetts. Shays and others like him throughout the United States were dissatisfied with the ineptitude of state legislatures during the economic depression after the American Revolution. Shays's Rebellion and other revolts spurred leading Americans to meet and discuss revising the **Articles of Confederation**.

Strict Constructionists

People such as **Thomas Jefferson** who believed that the Constitution forbade the government to take any actions that it did not expressly permit. The strict constructionists' interpretation was challenged by Alexander Hamilton and other **loose constructionists**, who believed that the Constitution allowed the government many implied powers.

Three-Fifths Clause

A nickname for Article I, Section II, Paragraph 3 of the Constitution, which states that representation in the House of Representatives is determined by counting all free persons and "three-fifths of all other persons," or slaves. The three-fifths clause was created as part of the **Great Compromise** between states with few slaves and those with many slaves.

Treaty of Ghent

The December 1814 treaty that ended the **War of 1812** between Britain and the United States. The treaty stated that the war had ended in a stalemate and that neither side had gained or lost any territory. Ironically, the **Battle of New Orleans**—the greatest American victory in the war—was fought about two weeks after the treaty had been signed, as General **Andrew Jackson** had not gotten word of the war's end.

Virginia and Kentucky Resolutions

Two resolutions, passed in 1798–1799 and written by **Thomas Jefferson** and **James Madison**, that declared that the individual states had the right to nullify unconstitutional acts of Congress. The resolutions stated that because the individual states had created the Union, they also reserved the right to nullify any legislation that ran counter to their interests.

Virginia Dynasty

A nickname that arose because four of the first five presidents (Washington, Jefferson, Madison, and Monroe) all hailed from Virginia. Many northern states resented this fact, as demonstrated by the **Hartford Convention**'s 1814 request that presidents should not come from the same state as their predecessor.

VIRGINIA PLAN

Also known as the **large state plan,** a proposal at the 1787 **Constitutional Convention** to create a **bicameral** (two-house) legislature in which delegates would be appointed according to the population of the state they represented. Large states with greater populations supported this plan, unlike small states, which backed the **New Jersey Plan** to create a unicameral legislature in which all states were equally represented. The **Great Compromise** solved the dilemma by creating a bicameral Congress featuring one house with proportional representation and another with equal representation.

WAR HAWKS

A younger generation of statesmen, primarily from the West and South, who replaced the Founding Fathers in the first decade of the 1800s. The War Hawks favored westward expansion and a nationalist agenda and thus encouraged war against both the **Northwest Confederacy** and against Britain (in the **War of 1812**). Despite their early zeal, many War Hawks, such as **Henry Clay,** eventually settled down to become some of the most revered statesmen in American history.

XYZ AFFAIR

A bribery scandal that caused public uproar during the Adams administration in 1798. After several naval skirmishes and French seizures of American merchant ships, Adams sent ambassadors to Paris to try to normalize relations. When the emissaries arrived, however, French officials demanded $250,000 before they would even speak with the Americans, let alone guarantee a truce. These officials, whom Adams dubbed X, Y, and Z, outraged Congress and the American public. Adams's popularity skyrocketed, and Congress braced for war. Although no war declaration was ever made, the United States and France waged undeclared naval warfare in the Atlantic for several years.

SUMMARY & ANALYSIS

THE ARTICLES OF CONFEDERATION: 1777–1787

EVENTS

1777	Congress is created under the Articles of Confederation
1781	Articles of Confederation is ratified
1785	Congress passes Land Ordinance of 1785
1787	Daniel Shays leads attack on federal arsenal at Springfield, Massachusetts Congress passes Northwest Ordinance of 1787

KEY PEOPLE

Thomas Jefferson Writer of the Declaration of Independence in 1776
Daniel Shays Disgruntled farmer who led a revolt against the Massachusetts state government in 1786–1787

THE ARTICLES OF CONFEDERATION

Shortly after **Thomas Jefferson** penned the **Declaration of Independence** in 1776, the delegates at the **Second Continental Congress** agreed that a new government was necessary to govern the now-independent colonies. After much debate, they drafted and adopted the **Articles of Confederation** in 1777.

Although the Articles were not officially ratified until 1781 (Maryland refused to ratify because of a territorial dispute), they served as the *de facto* constitution until that time. Under the authority of the Articles, the states created a national **Congress** comprised of annually elected delegates from all thirteen states. Each state had one vote in Congress, and, in most cases, decisions were made based on majority rule.

GOVERNMENT UNDER THE ARTICLES

The national Congress's powers over the states were specific and definite: it had the sole power to negotiate **treaties**, declare **war**, and make **peace**. It also reserved the right to maintain an **army and navy** and regulated interaction with **Native Americans** in the West. The delegates also granted Congress the power to resolve **interstate disputes**, grant **loans**, print **money**, and operate a national **postal system**. Eventually, Congress was also authorized to **govern western territories** until they achieved statehood.

All powers not granted to Congress were reserved for state governments. Congress had **no power to levy taxes,** for example. It could only request that the individual states raise revenue to cover their share of national expenses. Furthermore, any amendments made to the Articles required **unanimous agreement** from the states.

FEAR OF STRONG CENTRAL GOVERNMENT

The Articles made the national Congress weak on purpose. Having just won independence from Britain, many Americans feared that creating a strong federal government with too much authority over the states would only replace King George III with another tyrant. Instead, they envisioned Congress to be a supervisory body that would tie the states loosely for the common good. The early United States was thus a **confederation** of nearly independent states, not the solid federation with a strong government that it is today. The states were in many ways like individual countries bound together to keep Britain at bay.

Americans were especially afraid of **federal taxes**. Remembering the "No taxation without representation!" cry from the Colonial era, they stipulated that only the individual states could levy taxes. This system proved to be a completely ineffective way of bankrolling a federal government, and in fact, many of the states refused to pay their fair share. Most years, in fact, the Congress received less than a third of what it asked for from the states. Moreover, Congress had been granted **no rights to control interstate commerce**. States were thus given a free hand to draft conflicting and confusing laws that made cross-border trade difficult.

CONTINENTAL DOLLARS AND DEPRESSION

The new Congress immediately began printing **paper currency** to pay for the Revolutionary War. The money became the standard U.S. currency during the war, but when hard times hit and inflation skyrocketed, these Continental dollars became worthless. Many Americans, especially soldiers, small business owners, and farmers, were hit hard. Congress requested that the states increase taxes to help pay for a new national currency, but most states refused and instead printed their own paper money. This, too, succumbed to inflation, and by the end of the war, Americans had fistfuls of worthless money.

Western Land Disputes

Congress had much more success dealing with U.S. territories west of the Appalachians. Prior to the Revolutionary War, many of the original thirteen colonial legislatures made **territorial claims** to these lands. Interstate disputes over these western areas were common and heated: Maryland (which had no western claims) even refused to ratify the Articles of Confederation until the other states had ceded their claims. The conflict was resolved in 1781 when Virginia ceded all western lands to Congress's control so that all Americans could benefit from the land. Other states followed suit, and within a few years the national government was responsible for governing these territories.

Land Ordinance of 1785

Congress then passed the **Land Ordinance of 1785** to establish order in the West. The ordinance stipulated that new western towns were to be thirty-six miles square, with one square mile set aside for schools. All public lands were to be auctioned off to the highest bidders, providing all Americans the chance to migrate and settle in the West.

Northwest Ordinance of 1787

Later, Congress passed the **Northwest Ordinance of 1787** to establish a process for admitting these territories to the Union as states. Each territory was to be governed by Congress until it contained 5,000 free, white males. Then settlers could vote whether to become a permanent state on equal footing as all the other states in the Union.

The Northwest Ordinance also **abolished slavery in the territories** and granted freedom of religion and the right to trial by jury. Although the ordinance promised decent treatment to Native Americans, it did not, in reality, extend these rights to them. In fact, the United States obtained much of this land by extortion and violence against Native Americans.

Legacy of the Land Ordinances

These land ordinances were the only major successes that Congress had under the Articles. The Northwest Ordinance proved incredibly successful and influential because it allowed the small country to grow without devolving into an undemocratic empire. Unlike European powers that exploited their territories as colonies to be mined, Congress declared that all American territories could become **fully equal states** with the same status and privileges as the original founding states. In later years many Americans would interpret this to mean that it was their duty to expand democracy as far west as they could.

The Northwest Ordinance also sparked debate about the future of **slavery in the West**. A growing number of Americans during these years began to question the moral implications of slavery in a land where "all men were created equal." The ban on slavery in the Northwest Territories would prove to be the first of many restraints on the slaveholding South in the years leading up to the Civil War.

SHAYS'S REBELLION

Despite these successes in the West, many Americans were dissatisfied with life under the Articles of Confederation. **Economic depression** hit soon after the American Revolution ended, as many people, especially farmers, could not pay off their debts with the worthless state and Continental dollars. Most state legislatures refused to assist these impoverished farmers.

Increasingly angry, some of these farmers grabbed their muskets and marched their state capitals to redress grievances. The most notorious of these miniature revolts was **Shays's Rebellion** in Massachusetts, named after its Revolutionary War hero leader, Daniel Shays. Although officials in Boston quickly mustered a militia and quashed the rebellion, legislators nationwide agreed that change to the government was necessary if the United States were to survive.

A LANDMARK FAILURE

Despite its failures, the Articles of Confederation and the national Congress it created were landmarks in world history. The Articles were one of the first written constitutions in the world in which rights, duties, and powers of government and the people were expressly delineated for everyone to read.

Even though Congress, too, proved to be a failure, it was the first attempt in history to create a republican, representative government in a large country. Of course, the United States was not a true democracy at this time—every state still had voting restrictions that included women, blacks, Native Americans, and men without property—but the Articles were a bold first step.

CREATING THE CONSTITUTION: 1786–1787

EVENTS	
1786	Delegates from five states meet at Annapolis Convention to discuss revising Articles of Confederation
1787	Delegates from twelve states meet at Constitutional Convention in Philadelphia

KEY PEOPLE

George Washington Revolutionary War hero; chairman of the Constitutional Convention

THE ANNAPOLIS CONVENTION

To address the problems with the Articles of Confederation, delegates from five states met at the **Annapolis Convention** in Maryland in 1786. However, they could not agree on how these issues should be resolved. Finally, a new convention was proposed for the following year with the express purpose of revising the Articles of Confederation.

THE CONSTITUTIONAL CONVENTION

In 1787, delegates from twelve of the thirteen states (minus Rhode Island) met at the **Constitutional Convention** in Philadelphia. Most of the attendees were not die-hard revolutionaries (Thomas Jefferson, John Adams, Samuel Adams, and Patrick Henry were all absent). Nevertheless, most did have experience writing their own state constitutions. Though all fifty-five delegates involved in the proceedings were wealthy property owners, most were aware that they were serving a republic that comprised all social classes. **George Washington** was unanimously chosen as the chairman of the convention.

THREE BRANCHES OF GOVERNMENT

It quickly became clear to the Philadelphia delegates that the Articles should be scrapped and replaced with an entirely **new constitution** to create a stronger national government. Though this about-face was a violation of Congress's mandate to *revise* the Articles only, most delegates believed there was no other way to restore order in the Union.

The delegates began drafting a new **Constitution** to create a republican government. They decided on a government consisting of three branches: **legislative** (Congress), **executive** (the President), and **judicial** (headed by the Supreme Court). Delegates believed this **separation of powers** into three different branches would ensure that the United States would not become another monarchy.

SUMMARY & ANALYSIS

THE VIRGINIA AND NEW JERSEY PLANS

The structure of the new legislative branch was the subject of a heated debate, as delegates from Virginia and New Jersey both submitted proposals. The **Virginia Plan** called for a **bicameral** (two-house) legislature in which the number of representatives each state had would depend on the state's **population**. The larger, more populous states supported this proposal because it would give them more power. Hence, the Virginia plan came to be known as the **"large state plan."**

The **New Jersey Plan** proposed a **unicameral** (one-house) legislature in which all states had the same number of representatives regardless of population. This **"small state plan"** was, not surprisingly, the favorite of smaller states, which stood to gain power from it.

THE GREAT COMPROMISE

Eventually, the delegates settled on what came to be called the **Great Compromise**: a new Congress with two houses—an upper **Senate**, in which each state would be represented by two senators, and a lower **House of Representatives**, in which the number of delegates would be apportioned based on state population. Senators would be appointed by state legislatures every six years; representatives in the House would be elected directly by the people every two years.

Also, in the **three-fifths clause**, delegates agreed that each slave would be counted as three-fifths of a person when determining the population (and thus the number of representatives in the House) of each state.

THE PRESIDENT

The delegates had an easier time outlining presidential powers. Although some delegates had extreme opinions—Alexander Hamilton proposed a constitutional monarchy headed by an American king—most agreed that a new executive or **president** was needed to give the country the strong leadership that it had lacked under the Articles.

Article II of the Constitution thus outlined the powers of a new executive outside the control of Congress. The president would be elected via the **Electoral College** for a term of four years, would be **commander-in-chief** of the U.S. military, could **appoint judges**, and could **veto** legislation passed by Congress.

THE JUDICIARY

The judiciary branch of the new government would be headed by a **Supreme Court**, which would be headed by a **chief justice**. The structure of the rest of the federal court system, however, was not formalized until the Judiciary Act of 1789 (*see p. 31*).

CHECKS AND BALANCES

Many delegates felt that separation of powers was not enough to prevent one branch of government from dominating, so they also created a system of **checks and balances** to balance power even further. Under this system, each branch of government had the ability to check the powers of the others.

The president, for example, was given the power to **appoint** Supreme Court justices, cabinet members, and foreign ambassadors—but only with the approval of the Senate. On the other hand, the president was granted the right to **veto** all Congressional legislation.

Congress was given its own veto power over the president—a two-thirds majority vote could override any presidential veto. Congress also was charged with the responsibility to **confirm** presidential appointees—but also the power to block them. And finally, Congress had the ability to **impeach** and remove the president for treason, bribery, and other "high crimes and misdemeanors."

The Supreme Court was given the sweeping power of **judicial review**—the authority to declare an act of Congress unconstitutional and thereby strike it down.

FEAR OF PURE DEMOCRACY

The delegates also feared pure democracy and considered it to be the placement of the government directly in the hands of the "rabble." Many elements of the Constitution were thus engineered to ensure that only the "best men" would run the country.

Under the original Constitution, senators were to be **appointed** by state legislatures or governors, not elected by the people—in fact, this rule did not change until the Seventeenth Amendment (1913) established direct elections for senators. Although representatives in the House were elected directly by the people, their terms were set at only **two years**, compared to senators' six years. In addition, even though **new legislation** could be introduced only in the House, the Senate had to approve and ratify any bills before they could become law.

These checks on pure democracy were not confined to the legislative branch. The **Electoral College** was implemented to ensure that the uneducated masses didn't elect someone "unfit" for the presidency. **Life terms** for Supreme Court justices were also instituted as a safeguard against mob rule.

THE THREE-FIFTHS CLAUSE

Another point of contention arose over whether or how to count **slaves** in the U.S. population. Delegates from southern and mid-Atlantic slaveholding states wanted each slave to count as one full person in the census in order to increase their number of representatives in the House. Northern states, in which slaves made up a much lower percentage of the population, argued that slaves should not be counted at all.

After a long debate, both sides agreed on a **"three-fifths clause,"** which stated that each slave would count as three-fifths of a person. Delegates also agreed to permit international slave trading only for the next twenty years, until 1808. Nowhere in the original Constitution did the drafters use the word *slave*; instead, they used vague terms such as "other persons." Some historians have argued that this evasion indicates that slavery was polarizing Americans even in the late 1700s, well before the Civil War in the 1860s.

LEGACY OF THE CONSTITUTION

Political philosophers around the world hailed the Constitution as one of the most important documents in world history. It established the first stable democratic government and inspired the creation of similar constitutions around the world. Many modern historians, however, see the Constitution as a bundle of compromises rather than a self-conscious, history-altering document.

Indeed, as events over the next two years would prove, the new Constitution was highly controversial. When the Constitution was completed in September 1787, only thirty-nine of the original fifty-five delegates remained in Philadelphia and fully supported the new document. It was time to give the Constitution to the individual states for ratification.

The Federalist Papers and the Bill of Rights: 1788–1791

Events

1787	First Federalist Papers are published
1788	Nine states ratify the new Constitution
1789	George Washington becomes the first U.S. president
1791	Bill of Rights is ratified

Key People

Alexander Hamilton New York statesman who ardently supported the Constitution; coauthor of the Federalist Papers

James Madison Virginia lawyer; coauthor of the Federalist Papers; congressional sponsor of the Bill of Rights

John Jay New York lawyer; coauthor of the Federalist Papers; first chief justice of the Supreme Court

Ratification of the Constitution

The Articles of Confederation stipulated that all thirteen states had to **ratify** any new constitution for it to take effect. To circumvent this hurdle, the delegates included in the new Constitution a section outlining a new plan for ratification. Once nine of the thirteen states had ratified the document (at special conventions with elected representatives), the Constitution would replace the Articles in those nine states. The delegates figured correctly that the remaining states would be unable to survive on their own and would have to ratify the new document as well.

Federalists vs. Anti-Federalists

Debates erupted throughout the states about whether the new Constitution was an improvement. On one side were the **Federalists**, who favored the Constitution and a strong central government. The Federalists counted among their number many of the wealthier, propertied, and more educated Americans, including John Adams, George Washington, Benjamin Franklin, James Madison, and Alexander Hamilton, among others.

On the other side were the **Anti-Federalists**, who favored a weaker central government in favor of stronger state legislatures. Not all of them liked the Articles of Confederation, but none of them wanted the new Constitution to be ratified. Generally from the poorer classes in the West, but also with the support of patriots like Samuel Adams and Patrick Henry, the Anti-Federalists feared that a stronger national government would one day destroy the liberties Americans had won in the Revolution. They worried that the new Constitution didn't list any specific rights for the people.

A FEDERALIST VICTORY

Several of the **smaller states** quickly ratified the Constitution because it gave them more power in the new legislative branch than they had under the Articles of Confederation. Other ratifying conventions didn't end so quickly or peacefully. Riots broke out in several cities in 1787, and public debates between Federalists and Anti-Federalists were heated.

By mid-1788, nine states had ratified the Constitution, thus making it the new supreme law of the land in those nine states. Though the remaining four states—New York, Virginia, North Carolina, and Rhode Island—had Anti-Federalist majorities who hated the new Constitution, they knew they couldn't survive for long without the other nine states.

VIRGINIA, NORTH CAROLINA, AND RHODE ISLAND

Just as the final four states knew they couldn't survive without the other nine, the other nine realized they couldn't thrive without the final four. The Federalists had succeeded in putting the Constitution into effect, but they knew the new national government would lack legitimacy unless all the states were on board. Ardent Federalists campaigned for the Constitution in the remaining states, and in time, Virginia, North Carolina, and Rhode Island ratified it by narrow margins.

THE FEDERALIST PAPERS

The most difficult battle was waged in New York. Although New York eventually became the eleventh state to ratify the new Constitution, it was heavily Anti-Federalist, and victory was by no means assured at the outset.

In support of the Constitution, **Alexander Hamilton, James Madison,** and **John Jay** published a series of anonymous essays now known as the **Federalist Papers**. These propaganda essays extolled the benefits of a strong central government and allayed fears about civil liberties. Well written and persuasive, the essays are now regarded as some of the finest writings on American politics and republicanism.

Though many political philosophers in the 1700s had argued that republican government was impossible for large countries with diverse populations, the writers of the Federalist Papers argued the opposite. In their now-famous tenth essay (*Federalist No. 10*), Madison wrote that factionalism would not be a problem in a large republic precisely *because* everyone would have different interests. In other words, people would be so busy pursuing their own interests that emerging factions would cancel each other out, allowing freedom and republicanism to prevail.

THE FEDERALIST PAPERS AND NEW YORK

It's debatable whether the Federalist Papers had any significant impact on New York voters. Some historians point out that New Yorkers, like those in other states, based their votes on economic interests. Generally, those who stood to gain from a strong central government (such as merchants, shippers, and those who lived on the eastern seaboard) supported the Constitution, while those who would not gain (principally farmers) voted against it.

Perhaps more significant to New York State than the Federalist Papers was Alexander Hamilton's warning that the New York City government might secede from the state and join the Union on its own unless the state ratified the Constitution too.

THE BILL OF RIGHTS

Despite the Federalist Papers, most New Yorkers, North Carolinians, Virginians, and Rhode Islanders agreed to ratify the Constitution only if the document was amended to include a list of undeniable **rights and liberties** of the people. The new Congress kept its promise to do so and in 1791 established a committee to draft a **Bill of Rights**. Much of this work was done by **James Madison**, who sponsored the Bill of Rights in Congress. Congress added these rights to the Constitution as the first ten **amendments** later that year.

MAJOR AMENDMENTS

The **First Amendment** guarantees freedom of religion, speech, press, assembly, and petition. The **Second Amendment** protects the right to bear arms. The **Fifth** and **Sixth Amendments** guarantee the right of every person to trial by jury and safeguard the rights of the accused.

The **Ninth Amendment** stipulates that the Bill of Rights is not an exhaustive list and that the American people have rights beyond than those expressly stated in the Constitution. Finally, the **Tenth Amendment** states that all powers not granted to the new federal government are reserved for the individual states and the people.

WASHINGTON STRENGTHENS THE NATION: 1789–1792

EVENTS

1789	George Washington is elected president
	Congress passes the Judiciary Act of 1789
	French Revolution begins
1790	Congress creates Washington, D.C., as national capital
1791	Bank of the United States is founded
1792	Washington is reelected

KEY PEOPLE

George Washington First U.S. president; served two terms
John Adams Vice president to Washington
Alexander Hamilton First U.S. secretary of the treasury; advocated for creation of a Bank of the United States
Thomas Jefferson First U.S. secretary of state; argued against Hamilton's bank proposal

PRESIDENT WASHINGTON

In 1788, just months after the Constitution was ratified, **national elections** were held to choose representatives for the House of Representatives and the first U.S. president (senators were not elected directly by the people until 1913). Members of the **Electoral College** unanimously chose the war hero **George Washington** because of his popularity and keen leadership skills. Boston lawyer **John Adams** was chosen to be the first vice president.

THE FIRST CABINET

Though the Constitution states that the president "may require the opinion, in writing, of the principal officer in each of the executive departments," nowhere does it specifically mention a **cabinet** of advisors. Washington initially tried to gather advice as he needed it, but this method of consultation proved to be too confusing.

Eventually, Washington created a few executive officers (originally only the secretaries of state, war, and the treasury, and the attorney general) to meet with regularly. He chose **Thomas Jefferson** as secretary of state, **Alexander Hamilton** as secretary of the treasury, **Henry Knox** as secretary of war, and **Edmund Randolph** as attorney general. Washington's decision shaped the way that every one of his successors delegated executive authority.

WASHINGTON AS A SOUTHERNER

The fact that Washington was from the South was significant. Virginia had produced top-notch statesmen before the Revolution, and the trend continued well into the 1800s, as six of the first ten presidents were from Virginia. This **"Virginia Dynasty"** included Presidents Washington, Jefferson, Madison, Monroe, Harrison, and Tyler. More important, a southern president demonstrated to Americans and Europeans that the United States was in fact united. Despite differences between the North and South even at this early date, both regions were committed to maintaining a democratic Union. The 1790 decision to relocate the capital to **Washington, D.C.,** (*see* The Excise Tax, *p. 32*) reinforced this point.

THE JUDICIARY ACT OF 1789

Congress's first order of duty, even before ratifying the Bill of Rights, was to create the judiciary branch of government as stipulated by the Constitution. Thus, they passed the **Judiciary Act of 1789**, which established a **federal court system** with thirteen **district courts**, three **circuit courts**, and a **Supreme Court**—to be the highest court in the nation—presided over by six justices.

Congress did not want the federal court system to have too much power over local communities, so it determined that federal courts would serve primarily as **appeals courts** for cases already tried in state courts. In other words, most cases would first be heard by a judge in a local community, appealed to a state court, and finally appealed to the federal courts only if necessary.

HAMILTON'S REPORTS ON THE PUBLIC CREDIT

Secretary of the Treasury Alexander Hamilton, meanwhile, set out to establish firm financial policies for the country. In his famous *Reports on the Public Credit*, he proposed that the federal government should assume and pay off all **state debts**, as well as **federal debt**—a then-staggering sum in the tens of millions of dollars. Furthermore, Hamilton believed that the new government should sell **bonds** to encourage investment by citizens and foreign interests.

CONTROVERSY OVER NATIONAL DEBT

Hamilton wanted his measures to establish confidence in the new U.S. government at home and abroad. His proposal stipulated that Congress would have to fund the entire debt **at par**, which meant that the federal government would pay back all borrowed money *with* interest. Hamilton believed that funding the debt at par would

SUMMARY & ANALYSIS

send a signal that the United States was a responsible new member of the international community and a safe environment for speculators to invest their money. He also believed that a sizeable **national debt** would prevent states from drifting from the central government and thus bind them together.

However, Hamilton's ideas seemed ludicrous to many. Secretary of State Jefferson, for instance, believed that a large national debt would be a "national curse" that would depress poor farmers and ruin the economy. To the dismay of the Jeffersonians, assumption and funding at par both worked, as foreign investment began to boost the fledgling U.S. economy.

THE EXCISE TAX OF 1790

To raise money to pay off these debts, Hamilton suggested that Congress levy an **excise tax** on liquor. However, because farmers often converted their grain harvests into liquor before shipping (since liquor was cheaper to ship than grain), many congressmen from southern and western agrarian states believed that the excise tax was a scheme to make northern investors richer.

A compromise was finally reached in 1790: Congress would **assume all federal and state debts** and levy an **excise tax** to raise revenue. In exchange, the nation's capital would be moved from New York City to the new federal **District of Columbia** in the South.

THE BANK OF THE UNITED STATES

Hamilton then set out to create a national **Bank of the United States**, which would serve as a storehouse for federal money but also be funded by private investments. This proposal infuriated Secretary of State Jefferson and sparked even more of a debate than had the *Reports on the Public Credit.*

STRICT VS. LOOSE CONSTRUCTIONISM

Jefferson argued that creating a national bank would be unconstitutional because nowhere was it written in the Constitution that Congress had the authority to do so. He and his supporters were **"strict constructionists"**—they believed that the Constitution forbade everything it did not expressly permit.

Hamilton and most nationalistic Federalists, on the other hand, believed the opposite. These **"loose constructionists"** argued that the Constitution allowed everything it did not expressly forbid. President Washington agreed with Hamilton and signed the charter of the Bank of the United States in 1791.

THE CONSTITUTION ❦ 33

THE ELASTIC CLAUSE

The controversy over the national bank stemmed from differing interpretations of the Constitution's **"elastic clause,"** which grants Congress the power "to make all laws which shall be necessary and proper" to carry out its duties. Hamilton believed this clause justified creation of the national bank; Jefferson believed that the bank was unconstitutional and stripped power from the individual states.

HAMILTON'S REPORT ON MANUFACTURES

Hamilton also believed that the financial future of the United States depended on **manufacturing**, which at the time was meager and confined primarily to New England. Hamilton argued in his *Report on Manufactures* that building more factories and producing manufactured goods would make the nation rich and financially stable.

Jefferson again disagreed, believing that **agriculture** was the key to American success. Moreover, he felt that agrarian interests and farmers should form the foundations of any free republic in order to preserve liberty.

THE ROOTS OF POLITICAL PARTIES

The constant debates between Hamilton and Jefferson—and their own personal animosity for each other—split the cabinet and Congress during Washington's presidency and eventually led to the maturation of the Federalists and the Democratic-Republicans into distinct **political parties**. Though Federalist and Anti-Federalist factions had formed during the debate over ratification of the Constitution, neither were full-fledged political parties until Hamilton and Jefferson polarized political opinions in Congress and Washington's cabinet meetings.

At the time, political parties were looked down upon and viewed as undemocratic and even disloyal in the wake of the Revolution. Many, including Washington, believed that parties would only split the Union and destroy everything that Americans had worked so hard to achieve. Today, in contrast, political parties are regarded as essential components of any thriving democracy.

SUMMARY & ANALYSIS

WASHINGTON'S TROUBLES AT HOME AND ABROAD: 1790–1796

EVENTS

1790	First Indian Intercourse Act is passed
1793	Citizen Genêt affair causes outrage Washington issues Neutrality Proclamation
1794	Whiskey Rebellion is quashed Jay's Treaty is signed Battle of Fallen Timbers ends in Native American defeat
1795	Pinckney's Treaty is signed
1796	Washington reads Farewell Address

KEY PEOPLE

John Jay Supreme Court chief justice who negotiated Jay's Treaty with Britain
George Washington First U.S. president; advocated neutrality; warned against factionalism
Citizen Genêt French ambassador who violated Washington's Neutrality Proclamation

TENSIONS WITH NATIVE AMERICANS

Problems in the West plagued Washington during his presidency. Since the end of the French and Indian War, American settlers had pushed farther and farther westward into the **Ohio Valley**. Although the Land Ordinance of 1785 and Northwest Ordinance of 1787 paid lip service to the notion that Native Americans should receive fair treatment from settlers, little was done to ensure that this was the case. By the end of the eighteenth century, relations between settlers and Native Americans, who were angry that they received no compensation for their lands, were tense.

In 1790, Congress passed the first of the **Indian Intercourse Acts** to resolve the situation peacefully. These acts stipulated that the United States would regulate all trade with Native Americans and that it would acquire new lands in the West only via official **treaties**. In reality, the acts had little real weight; most American farmers ignored them, and bloody clashes continued. Ultimately, settlers gained the upper hand after U.S. forces routed many of the most powerful tribes at the **Battle of Fallen Timbers** in 1794.

Many whites generally looked down on Native Americans as savages who didn't use the land properly; as a result, they had few qualms about taking native lands. Meanwhile, Democratic-Republicans and their expansionist Jacksonian successors usually turned a blind eye to the suffering of Native Americans in the hopes of winning the support of more rural supporters.

THREATS FROM SPAIN

Washington also felt pressure in the West from **Spain**, which controlled the **Louisiana Territory** and **Florida** and areas from British Canada north of the Ohio Valley. Spain was highly suspicious of the new United States and feared that American settlers' thirst for new western lands would prompt Congress to annex portions of Spanish territory.

As a result, Spain denied American farmers access to the **Mississippi River**, which was necessary for shipping grain to the East via the Gulf of Mexico and the Atlantic. They also allied themselves with many Native American tribes in the region.

THREATS FROM BRITAIN

Britain also feared American expansion. Although the Treaty of Paris that had ended the Revolutionary War stipulated that the **Ohio Valley** was American territory, British troops remained stationed in the region to protect their old trade interests. They also feared another attempt to invade Canada. Worse, however, was the British navy's continued seizure of American trade ships and cargos in the Caribbean and Atlantic.

THE FRENCH REVOLUTION

Few other international events had such a profound impact on the United States as the **French Revolution**, which began in 1789 when the French overthrew King Louis XVI. Thomas Jefferson and many other Americans rejoiced that the French were continuing the revolutionary cause to plant democracy in Europe. Jefferson believed that a firm friendship with republican France would benefit both countries.

However, when the revolution turned bloody, heads (literally) began to roll, and war erupted between France and Britain, American public opinion became split. Though most of Jefferson's supporters believed the United States should still honor the 1778 Franco-American alliance, more conservative Americans, such as Alexander Hamilton, thought the United States should seek an alliance with London.

WASHINGTON'S NEUTRALITY PROCLAMATION

After a heated debate over whether the United States should ally itself with France or Britain, Washington finally ended the debate when he issued his **Neutrality Proclamation** in 1793. The proclamation pledged mutual friendship and the desire to trade with both nations.

THE CITIZEN GENÊT AFFAIR

The neutrality issue was not closed for the French, however. France's ambassador to the United States, **Edmond Genêt** (or Citizen Genêt, as he preferred to be called), violated Washington's neutrality order by commissioning U.S. privateers to fight for France and trying to make arrangements to use U.S. ports in the war effort against Britain. The **Citizen Genêt affair**, as it came to be called, caused such outrage that Genêt was recalled as ambassador. He chose to remain in the country, however, and ultimately even became a U.S. citizen. Jefferson, displeased and embarrassed by Genêt, eventually resigned his cabinet post, in part over the affair.

THE WHISKEY REBELLION

The domestic turbulence and foreign clashes of the late 1780s caused many Americans to grow discontented with their new government—a problem that was only exacerbated by the passage of Hamilton's **excise tax** in 1790. Because most farmers converted their grain harvests to alcohol before shipping, the tax placed a heavy burden on their already-empty pocketbooks.

In reaction, a small band of Pennsylvania farmers initiated the **Whiskey Rebellion** against the government in 1794 to redress grievances and seek change. Rumors of insurrection and another revolution circulated from the West, through the countryside, until they reached lawmakers in Philadelphia. In response, Washington organized an army of 13,000 and marched them to western Pennsylvania. Upon arrival, however, the troops found that the shocked and awed rebels had already disbanded. This first true test of the new federal government did much to demonstrate Washington's willpower and the government's authority.

JAY'S TREATY

To prevent another war with Britain, Washington dispatched Chief Justice of the Supreme Court **John Jay** to London in 1794 to negotiate a settlement. Under **Jay's Treaty**, Britain agreed to withdraw its troops from the Ohio Valley and pay damages for American ships that the Royal Navy had seized illegally. The United States, meanwhile, agreed to pay outstanding pre-Revolutionary War debts. The treaty greatly displeased the Jeffersonians, who believed that the United States was cozying up to Britain and thought the treaty required horrendous concessions.

PICKNEY'S TREATY

A year later, in 1795, **Pinckney's Treaty** ended the disputes with Spain. The agreement gave Americans access to the Mississippi River in exchange for promises of nonaggression against Spanish territory in the West. Hamiltonians disapproved of this treaty as much as the Jeffersonians disapproved of Jay's Treaty. The two sides compromised by ratifying both treaties.

WASHINGTON'S FAREWELL ADDRESS

Tired of the demands of the presidency, Washington declined to run for a third term, and in 1796, he read his **Farewell Address** to the nation. In the speech, he urged Americans not to become embroiled in European affairs. In response to the growing political battles between Jefferson and Hamilton, he also warned against the dangers of **factionalism** and stated his belief that political parties would ruin the nation.

SUMMARY & ANALYSIS

THE ADAMS PRESIDENCY: 1797–1800

SUMMARY & ANALYSIS

EVENTS

1796	John Adams is elected second president
1797	XYZ Affair occurs
1798	Congress passes Alien and Sedition Acts United States wages undeclared naval war with France Virginia Resolutions written
1799	Kentucky Resolutions written

KEY PEOPLE

John Adams Second U.S. president; approved controversial Alien and Sedition Acts
Thomas Jefferson Vice president under Adams; major Democratic-Republican figure; coauthor of Virginia and Kentucky Resolutions
James Madison Coauthor of Virginia and Kentucky Resolutions

SOLIDIFICATION OF POLITICAL PARTIES

By the end of Washington's second term, the ideological and personal differences between Hamilton and Jefferson had spread to politicians nationwide. The Hamiltonians coalesced into the **Federalists**—loose constructionists who favored a strong national government over the states, a solid economy based on manufacturing, and improved relations with Britain.

The Jeffersonians coalesced into the **Democratic-Republicans**—strict constructionists who feared a centralized government, supported the development and expansion of agriculture, and were generally pro-France.

THE ELECTION OF 1796

Because rivalry between the Federalists and Democratic-Republicans had intensified, the **election of 1796** was quite heated, unlike either of the previous presidential elections. Debates in Congress were passionate and sometimes even bloody, as was the case when one Federalist attacked a Democratic-Republican with a cane, only to be struck back with a fireplace poker.

Washington's vice president, **John Adams**, became the Federalist candidate, while Thomas Jefferson ran for the Democratic-Republicans. Adams received more Electoral College votes than Jefferson and thus became president. However, under the original Constitution, the candidate with the second-highest number of electoral votes—in this case, Jefferson—became vice president. Consequently, Adams was left saddled with a vice president from the opposing party. The presence of a Democratic-Republican so high up in the Adams administration made it difficult at times for the president to promote his Federalist agenda.

Undeclared Warfare with France

The first test of Adams's mettle came from France in 1796, when Paris ended all diplomatic relations with the United States in response to Jay's Treaty of the previous year. Having expected the United States to uphold the Franco-American alliance of 1778, France had been stunned when Washington issued the Neutrality Proclamation, then further stunned when Jay's Treaty had normalized relations with Britain. The French navy began to seize hundreds of American ships and millions of dollars worth of cargo without cause or compensation.

The XYZ Affair

Adams, wanting to avoid open war with France, sent ambassadors to Paris in 1797 to negotiate peace and normalize relations. When the emissaries arrived, however, French officials demanded a $250,000 bribe before they would even speak with the Americans, let alone guarantee a truce. These officials, whom Adams dubbed X, Y, and Z, outraged Congress and the American public. The **XYZ Affair** prompted many to cry, "Millions for defense, but not one cent for tribute!"

Adams's popularity skyrocketed, and Congress braced for war. Although no war declaration was ever made, the United States and France waged undeclared naval warfare in the Atlantic for several years. Shortly before he left office several years later, Adams negotiated an end to the fighting: in exchange for ignoring damages to seized cargos, France agreed to annul the Franco-American alliance.

The Alien and Sedition Acts

Adams's sudden boost in popularity gave him and the Federalist-controlled Congress the confidence to make the federal government even stronger. In an attempt to prevent French immigrants from making trouble within the United States in the event of a war with France, Congress in 1798 passed the **Alien Acts**, which extended the residency time required for foreigners to become American citizens from five years to fourteen years and gave the president the power to expel any aliens who were considered to be dangerous.

In the hopes of seriously weakening or eliminating the Democratic-Republicans, Congress also passed the **Sedition Act** in the same year, which banned all forms of public expression critical of the president or Congress.

DEMOCRATIC-REPUBLICAN REACTION

The Alien and Sedition Acts kicked the Democratic-Republican opposition into high gear despite the fact that the laws were intended to silence them. They considered the laws unrepublican and an affront to their First-Amendment right to free speech. For the first time, the Democratic-Republicans began to organize as a true **opposition party** in Congress: they formed **caucuses**, selected **party leaders**, and outlined a **platform**. They also challenged Federalists for the office of Speaker of the House, which previously had been a nonpartisan position.

This growing opposition only made the Federalists angrier and even more determined to ruin their opponents. Not surprisingly, the growing power struggle in Congress produced heated debates and even a few fistfights. In the most notorious fight, two Congressmen attacked each other with a cane and a hot fire poker.

THE VIRGINIA AND KENTUCKY RESOLUTIONS

Vice President Jefferson and James Madison, even bolder in their opposition to the Alien and Sedition Acts, anonymously drafted the **Virginia and Kentucky Resolutions**, which proclaimed the Alien and Sedition Acts null and void in those states. The Resolutions argued that the Constitution was a contract among states and that when Congress violated that contract by passing unconstitutional legislation, the individual states reserved the right to **nullify** it.

The Resolutions were two of the most influential American political works prior to the Civil War. Arguing that member states had the authority to nullify unconstitutional acts of Congress, the resolutions effectively claimed the power of **judicial review** for the states, not the Supreme Court. The resolutions also sparked the first debate over whether the states or the federal government had the final authority.

Future Democrats—the political descendents of the Democratic-Republicans—would continue this line of reasoning later in U.S. history. One example was John C. Calhoun, whose "South Carolina Exposition" essay sparked the Nullification Crisis of 1832–1833, which contributed toward support for southern secession and the Civil War.

THE FEDERALIST LEGACY

In the years between the ratification of the Constitution and James Madison's presidency, the system of two-party politics in the United States began, with political loyalties split between the Democratic-Republicans and Federalists. The Adams presidency marked the peak of the Federalist Party. John Adams was the first and only Federalist president, and the party largely dissipated by the end of the War of 1812.

Even though Federalism was short-lived, it had a profound impact on American history. Federalism helped create a strong Union, strengthened the office of the presidency, put the nation on solid financial footing, and established the authority of the Supreme Court.

JEFFERSON'S AGRARIAN REPUBLIC:
1800–1808

EVENTS

1800	Thomas Jefferson is elected president
1803	Louisiana Purchase is finalized Supreme Court issues *Marbury v. Madison* ruling
1804	Jefferson is reelected Louis and Clark begin exploration of Louisiana Territory
1807	British warship seizes USS *Chesapeake* Congress passes Embargo Act

KEY PEOPLE

John Adams Second U.S. president; made controversial last-minute judicial appointments
Thomas Jefferson Third U.S. president; promoted agrarian interests and wanted to limit
    federal government power
John Marshall Supreme Court chief justice; issued landmark *Marbury v. Madison* ruling

SUMMARY & ANALYSIS

THE CONTESTED ELECTION OF 1800

The fallout from the Alien and Sedition Acts dealt a serious blow to John Adams and the Federalists. Despite the Sedition Act's attempt to suppress free speech, Democratic-Republicans rallied around the Virginia and Kentucky Resolutions. Also damaging to the Federalists was the internal power struggle between the president and Alexander Hamilton. The two had been opponents within the Federalist Party for years but cut all ties with each other when Adams chose to negotiate peace with the French in 1800. The ideological rift split the party in two and ruined Adams's chances for reelection.

In the **election of 1800**, Thomas Jefferson and New Yorker **Aaron Burr**—both Democratic-Republicans—received the same number of Electoral College votes. The Federalist Congress therefore had to determine which of their hated rivals would become the next president. After much debate, Congress chose **Thomas Jefferson.**

THE "REVOLUTION OF 1800"

Despite the viciousness of the campaign, there were no revolts or riots when the Democratic-Republicans took office. Such a peaceful transition of power from one party to another was almost unprecedented in history. Indeed, many historians call the election of 1800 the **"Revolution of 1800"**—a crucial moment that confirmed that the new nation would survive. Contemporary Europeans who had believed that the "American experiment" would ultimately fail were also temporarily quieted.

Jefferson's Small Government

As a strict constructionist, Jefferson believed in **limited federal government** and, as a result, worked immediately to decrease the size of the government after taking office. He made cuts to the army and navy, reduced the number of federal employees, and strove to eliminate the national debt. He felt that most powers should be reserved for the individual states. These policies ran contrary to all Federalist beliefs in a strong centralized government.

Jefferson the Agrarian

Jefferson received most of his support in the election from the South and from the western frontier, undoubtedly because the Virginian portrayed himself as an advocate of the farmer and common man. Indeed, approximately eighty percent of Americans at this time were farmers. Although some farmed **cash crops** to resell, the vast majority lived on family farms and grew food for their own **subsistence**. They built their own houses, raised their own animals, grew their own food, and made their own clothes.

Jefferson firmly believed that these men and women were the heart of American republicanism and that the future of the nation rested upon their shoulders. He abhorred the squalor and gross inequality he saw in the developing factory cities in Europe and wanted to avoid the same inequality in the United States.

Adams's Midnight Justices

Nevertheless, Adams did attempt to seek revenge. During his last days as president, he created several new judiciary positions and filled the posts with Federalist supporters. Jefferson and his secretary of state, James Madison, refused to honor the appointments of these **"midnight justices."**

Marbury v. Madison

One of the justices, **William Marbury**, sued Madison for his appointment, and the case eventually reached the Supreme Court in 1803. Chief Justice **John Marshall**, a die-hard Federalist, sympathized with Marbury but believed that Jefferson would never adhere to a ruling against Madison. Therefore, Marshall ruled in *Marbury v. Madison* that although Marbury was entitled to the judgeship, the Supreme Court could not force the president to give it to him.

Although the Judiciary Act of 1789 had given the Supreme Court this power, Marshall's ruling effectively declared that act unconstitutional. Marshall thus simultaneously gave Jefferson his victory and strengthened the Supreme Court with the power of **judicial review**—the right to declare Congress's laws unconstitutional.

THE LOUISIANA PURCHASE

Despite his belief in limited government, Jefferson seized the opportunity in 1803 to buy the vast expanse of the **Louisiana Territory** from France. France had reacquired the territory from Spain in 1801, but Napoleon's costly war in Europe forced him to consider selling the land. Jefferson, fearing that the French would revoke U.S. access to the major Mississippi River port of New Orleans, sent **James Monroe** to Paris to offer $10 million for New Orleans alone. Napoleon, however, in need of money, offered the entire Louisiana Territory for $15 million, and Monroe agreed.

Although the Constitution said nothing about the purchase of new lands, Jefferson swallowed his pride and accepted the **Louisiana Purchase**. The new territories included present-day Louisiana, Arkansas, Missouri, Minnesota, North Dakota, South Dakota, Nebraska, and Kansas, as well as parts of Montana, Wyoming, Colorado, and Oklahoma—all for a mere $15 million. Not only was the purchase the best real estate deal in history by far, it also established a precedent for purchasing lands to expand the United States farther westward.

LEWIS AND CLARK'S EXPEDITION

In 1804, Jefferson dispatched his secretary **Meriwether Lewis** and army captain **William Clark** to explore the Louisiana Territory. Lewis and Clark's famous two-year expedition to the Pacific helped publicize the bountiful new lands. In addition to finding countless natural wonders in the West, the pair traversed the fertile Mississippi Valley, which Jefferson hoped would become the heartland of an agrarian United States.

ANGLO-AMERICAN TENSIONS

Relations with Britain soured during Jefferson's years in office. When war broke out between Britain and Napoleonic France after the turn of the century, neutral American merchants made huge profits shipping food, supplies, and natural resources to both countries. The British Royal Navy, still the dominant world naval power, began to seize American ships and cargos bound for France in 1805.

Moreover, the British navy also began **impressing** U.S. sailors for forced servitude on British war ships. Though Britain claimed that they impressed only deserters from the Royal Navy, it is estimated that Britain actually took more than 5,000 Americans illegally.

THE EMBARGO ACT

When the British warship **HMS *Leopard*** entered American territorial waters and impressed several Americans from the merchant ship **USS *Chesapeake*** in 1807, Jefferson was outraged. Fed up with Britain's and France's refusal to accept U.S. sovereignty, Jefferson convinced Congress to pass the Embargo Act that same year to punish both nations.

The **Embargo Act** forbade American ships from sailing to all foreign ports until Britain and France agreed to respect American shipping rights. Jefferson's plan backfired, however, for he failed to realize that American merchants needed trade with Europe more than European merchants needed trade with America. Economic **depression** struck the United States very hard, but Jefferson refused to rescind the Embargo Act even when it became evident that it was failing. The act was repealed only in 1809, two days before Jefferson left office.

JEFFERSON'S LEGACY

All in all, Jefferson was much more successful as a statesman during the American Revolution and as Washington's secretary of state than as president. On one hand, he established several key precedents, such as the purchase of new lands to expand the United States. On the other hand, his Embargo Act and his repeal of Hamilton's excise tax ran the country into the ground economically.

Fortunately for Jefferson's reputation, the long-term benefits of the Louisiana Purchase far outweighed the disastrous effects of the economic depression. Also important was the foundation he laid for **democracy** and **agrarianism** that the Jacksonian Democrats would later build upon to expand democracy.

MADISON AND THE WAR OF 1812: 1808–1815

EVENTS

1808	James Madison is elected president
1809	Tecumseh unites Native Americans in Mississippi basin Congress repeals Embargo Act Congress passes Non-Intercourse Act
1810	Congress passes Macon's Bill No. 2
1811	William Henry Harrison defeats pan-Indian alliance at Battle of Tippecanoe
1812	Madison is reelected War of 1812 begins
1814	New Englanders meet at Hartford Convention Treaty of Ghent ends war
1815	Andrew Jackson defeats British forces at Battle of New Orleans

KEY PEOPLE

James Madison Fourth U.S. president; promoted southern and western agriculture and led the United States in the War of 1812

Tecumseh Head of Native American Northwest Confederacy; his forces were defeated at the Battle of Tippecanoe in 1811

William Henry Harrison Former Indiana governor and army general; defeated the Northwest Confederacy at Tippecanoe

Andrew Jackson Tennessee military hero of the Battle of New Orleans and Creek War

THE ELECTION OF 1808

The depression stemming from Jefferson's Embargo Act weakened the Democratic-Republicans in the election of 1808. Although **James Madison** was still able to defeat Federalist candidate Charles Pinckney easily for the presidency, the Democratic-Republicans lost seats in Congress. As Jefferson's chosen successor, Madison continued to carry out his fellow Virginian's policies throughout both of his presidential terms.

THE NON-INTERCOURSE ACT

Congress's first order of business in 1809 was to repeal the hated and ineffective Embargo Act, which had prevented U.S. ships from sailing to foreign ports. Congress replaced this act with the **Non-Intercourse Act**, which banned trade only with Britain and France until both agreed to respect American sovereignty and shipping rights.

MACON'S BILL NO. 2

The following year, Congress, in a further attempt to revive the faltering U.S. economy, passed **Macon's Bill No. 2**, which restored U.S.

trade relations with Britain and France but promised to reinstate the Non-Intercourse Act if either nation violated U.S. shipping rights.

Tecumseh and the Northwest Confederacy

Madison's term was fraught with troubled Native American relations, as white settlers began to pour into the Louisiana Purchase and steal native lands, ignoring the Indian Intercourse Acts of the 1790s. When Congress seemed unwilling to do anything about the situation, two Shawnee brothers, **Tecumseh** and **Tenskwatawa** (also commonly called the Prophet), tried to unite all of the tribes in the Mississippi Valley region against the settlers. Preaching a return to traditional ways of life, Tecumseh and The Prophet were highly successful and created the **Northwest Confederacy** that included the Shawnee, Cherokee, Choctaw, Chickasaw, and Creek tribes, among others.

The Battle of Tippecanoe

Congress, fearing a Native American uprising, ordered the governor of the Indiana Territory, **William Henry Harrison**, to disband the Northwest Confederacy. Indeed, Harrison soundly defeated the Confederacy at the **Battle of Tippecanoe** in 1811.

The War Hawks

By the 1810s, many of the older and more experienced representatives and senators in Congress had been replaced by young and passionate new faces. It was these hotheaded **"War Hawks,"** primarily from southern and western states, who had ordered Harrison to take military action against the Northwest Confederacy. As frontiersmen-politicians, the War Hawks were strongly expansionist, and the Confederacy offered the perfect excuse to drive Native Americans even further west.

The War Hawks also clamored for a new war against Britain, citing Britain's impressment of U.S. sailors, seizure of American ships and cargos, and refusal to withdraw troops from the Louisiana Territory. The War Hawks also hoped that victory in a new war would win Canada— and perhaps even Florida, if Spain tried to help Britain—for the United States. Although President Madison hoped to avoid war, he eventually caved to pressures from the War Hawks and requested that Congress declare war against Britain in June of 1812.

The War of 1812

In many ways, the war went badly for the United States. As a result of Jefferson's belief in frugal government, the U.S. Navy had been pared down to only a few gunboats, and the Army was similarly

SUMMARY & ANALYSIS

meager. Though American forces had some success in the North-west, they were unable to push through the British blockade of the eastern ports or prevent the **burning of Washington, D.C.,** in 1814. For most of 1814, the war remained a stalemate.

THE HARTFORD CONVENTION

The War of 1812 did not have nationwide support: the South and West supported it, but the New England states, whose economies depended on shipping with Europe, voted against the war in Congress and protested loudly against it once it began. In fact, five of the New England states were so fervently opposed to the war that they convened a secret meeting in Hartford, Connecticut, to discuss secession from the Union.

After several weeks of discussion, delegates at the **Hartford Convention** nixed the idea of secession and instead decided merely to petition Congress to redress a list of grievances. First, they wanted the U.S. government to **compensate New England shippers** for lost profits. Second, they wanted to **amend the Constitution** so that the states could vote on important decisions that affected the entire Union, such as admission of new states or declaration of war. Third, they wanted to **change the executive office** so that each president could serve only one term and no two consecutive presidents could come from the same state (primarily out of frustration that most presidents had come from the South). Finally, they wanted to **strike the three-fifths clause from the Constitution**.

THE TREATY OF GHENT

Unfortunately for the Hartford delegates, their petition arrived in Washington too late, just after news broke that the war had ended. Britain and the United States, weary of being stuck in a costly conflict that was more or less a stalemate, had signed the **Treaty of Ghent** to end hostilities. The treaty essentially stipulated that neither side had gained or lost any territory, and it made no mention of impressments or the illegal seizure of ships. For obvious reasons, none of the Hartford Convention's demands were granted.

THE BATTLE OF NEW ORLEANS

Oddly, the most famous battle of the War of 1812 was fought two weeks after the peace treaty was signed. General **Andrew Jackson**, who had not yet received word of the treaty, led U.S. troops to a resounding victory in early January 1815 at the **Battle of New Orleans**.

LEGACY OF THE WAR OF 1812

Despite the sectional divides and the overall futility of the war, the United States emerged from the War of 1812 with a newfound sense of enthusiasm and national pride. Though the nation had neither lost nor gained territory, Jackson's smashing victory at New Orleans gave the nation a previously unknown feeling of confidence. To Americans, the battle proved once and for all that the United States was an independent nation, not just a rogue colony. For this reason, many historians refer to the War of 1812 as America's second war for independence.

SUMMARY & ANALYSIS

STUDY QUESTIONS & ESSAY TOPICS

Always use specific historical examples to support your arguments.

STUDY QUESTIONS

1. *How effective was the national Congress under the Articles of Confederation? Why were the Articles replaced by the Constitution? How was the federal government different under the Constitution?*

Afraid of strong centralized government after the Revolutionary War, the drafters of the Articles of Confederation made certain that the federal government would never be able to strip power from the individual states. As a result, the national Congress was so weak and politically ineffective that it was unable to maintain national unity and went virtually bankrupt. The specter of rebellion and collapse forced American elites to create a stronger, more centralized government under the Constitution.

In 1777, America's leading politicians were well aware that powerful governments could become stifling and oppressive. In the Declaration of Independence, Thomas Jefferson had outlined King George III's "long train of abuses" against the colonies: unfair and unpopular taxes, quartering acts, and other punishments. With these abuses fresh in mind, the framers of the Articles decided that the United States should be only a loose confederation of thirteen nearly independent members. They believed that this structure would bind the states for common defense but would allow republicanism to flourish in smaller communities. The Articles therefore created a national Congress with the power to maintain armies, declare war and peace, govern western lands, and resolve interstate disputes, but lacking the power to levy direct taxes. Each state was given one vote, and most decisions were to be made by majority rule.

Although the confederation looked good on paper, it proved to be wholly ineffective. First, Congress had virtually no power to control the states. Commerce and territorial disputes erupted throughout the decade during which the Articles were in effect. Second,

Congress, unable to levy taxes of its own, could only request money from the individual states. Many states, however, refused to pay. Finally, growing domestic unrest among the working classes, which reached a peak in Shays's Rebellion, convinced wealthier Americans that the Articles had to be amended, if not replaced.

Under the new Constitution, the United States was a more tightly bound federation than the loose confederation that had existed under the Articles. The new federal government was divided into three separate but equal branches, each with distinct powers and authority. The new bicameral Congress was given the power to levy taxes, while the president was given the authority to execute and enforce congressional laws. The Supreme Court assumed the task of judicial review to determine whether Congress's laws were constitutional. Thus, though the Constitution gave the new government greater power and authority, it also instituted safeguards to keep federal power in check, as the framers of the Articles of Confederation had originally intended.

2.   *Which political group do you believe had a more profound effect on the formation of the United States, the Federalists or the Democratic-Republicans?*

Even though Democratic-Republican presidents held the White House for twenty-four of the United States' first thirty-six years, the Federalists had a much greater effect on the formation of the new nation. The Federalists pushed for the ratification of the Constitution and then bolstered the federal government by providing solid economic and legal infrastructure. Their influence put in place the systems that have kept the United States stable and unified throughout its history.

Had the Anti-Federalists had their way, the Constitution might never have been ratified. Patriots like Patrick Henry and Samuel Adams believed that the new federal government would be too powerful and too constricting. They feared that the new office of president was too much like a monarch and did not think that Congress should have the right to tax all Americans. Like many political philosophers of their day, they thought that republicanism would never survive in a large country because the government would be too distant from the hearts and minds of the people it represented.

Federalists, however, disagreed. In the Federalist Papers, Alexander Hamilton, John Jay, and James Madison argued that republi-

QUESTIONS & ESSAYS

canism would work for the United States. The republic would be so large, with so many conflicting constituencies, that no single faction would ever be able to dominate the others. Moreover, safeguards inserted into the Constitution, such as the separation of powers and the system of checks and balances, would prevent the government from ever becoming too powerful. These Federalist arguments helped convince the states to ratify the Constitution.

Other major Federalist contributions came through Secretary of the Treasury Alexander Hamilton's economic policies, which bolstered the federal government and put the nation on sound financial footing. Despite protests from Thomas Jefferson and other Democratic-Republicans, Hamilton urged President Washington and Congress to support the development of American manufacturing, pass an excise tax to fund the government, assume all state and federal debts, fund those debts at par, and create a Bank of the United States. The assumption of debt and funding at par gave the country credibility and encouraged speculators to invest in American enterprises. The excise tax filled the federal treasury, and the Bank of the United States helped stabilize the economy. Perhaps most important, the Federalists' loose interpretation of the Constitution justified strong centralized government.

The Federalists also influenced the U.S. legal infrastructure through the decisions of Chief Justice of the Supreme Court John Marshall. Most of Marshall's rulings during his years as chief justice bolstered the federal government's power vis-à-vis the individual states. In *Marbury v. Madison*, for example, he secured the power of judicial review for the Supreme Court. In subsequent cases, he also defended the Court's superior position to state courts. In doing so, Marshall legitimized the federal government and gave it strong legal precedents.

3.   *Which nation was responsible for the War of 1812,
      Britain or the United States? What caused the war?*

Despite the fact that the United States was the first to declare war, Britain clearly initiated the conflict, as British troops continued to occupy U.S. territory in the Ohio Valley and the Royal Navy seized American merchant ships and impressed their crews. The United States tried to resolve the disputes diplomatically, and then, when diplomatic attempts failed, imposed trade sanctions on Britain in an attempt to gain London's attention. However, these measures failed, leaving President James Madison and Congress little choice but to defend American sovereignty.

The war stemmed from the fact that Britain had continued to treat the United States as one of its colonies even after the Revolutionary War and the establishment of a new U.S government. Under the Treaty of Paris, Britain had agreed to withdraw its troops from the Ohio Valley and to respect American shipping. In practice, though, neither promise was ever honored: British troops remained stationed in British forts on U.S. territory, and Royal Navy captains continued to seize American merchant ships. The British made the same concessions again in Jay's Treaty in 1794 but never honored those commitments either. In fact, seizures of American merchant ships increased in the first decade of the 1800s, and Royal Navy officers began to impress an increasing number of American sailors to serve on British warships. Impressment outraged Americans and thus forced the U.S. government to act.

When diplomatic efforts failed to resolve the crisis peacefully, Jefferson encouraged Congress to pass the Embargo Act in 1807 to ban trade with all foreign countries. Jefferson hoped the sanctions would convince the British government to change its ways. Unfortunately, the implementation of the Embargo Act failed miserably and only hurt American merchants. Congress repealed the law in 1809 and tried to use the new Non-Intercourse Act to ban trade only with Britain and France. This act, however, likewise failed to produce any response, leaving Congress effectively out of diplomatic options.

QUESTIONS & ESSAYS

SUGGESTED ESSAY TOPICS

1. *How did the Anti-Federalists help shape the United States?*

2. *Did the "elastic clause" justify acts such as Hamilton's excise tax and Bank of the United States or Jefferson's Louisiana Purchase?*

3. *How would you characterize Anglo-British relations in the years after independence?*

4. *Describe how three of the following affected the formation of the federal government:*

   a) Marbury v. Madison
   b) the Louisiana Purchase
   c) the Bank of the United States
   d) the Alien and Sedition Acts

5. *Was the Constitution written to be a self-consciously landmark document or was it simply a compilation of compromises? Support your argument.*

REVIEW & RESOURCES

QUIZ

1. The Articles of Confederation granted Congress all of the following powers *except*

   A. The power to conduct foreign relations
   B. The power to levy taxes
   C. The power to maintain armed forces
   D. The power to resolve disputes among the states

2. The Land Ordinance of 1785

   A. Guaranteed certain rights and liberties to western settlers
   B. Was passed after Shays's Rebellion threatened the security of eastern cities
   C. Established an orderly system for surveying land in the West
   D. Allowed Native Americans to sell their land to the United States

3. Why did Daniel Shays attack the federal arsenal in Springfield, Massachusetts, with 1,200 men in 1787?

   A. He wanted the legislature to offer relief to impoverished debtors
   B. He was protesting the Land Ordinance of 1785
   C. He was protesting the Articles of Confederation
   D. He did not want the Constitution to be ratified

4.   How was the government under the Constitution different from that under the Articles of Confederation?

    A.   Congress had the authority to declare war under the Articles but not under the Constitution

    B.   Congress had the power to levy taxes under the Constitution but not under the Articles

    C.   The president was the commander-in-chief of the armed forces under the Articles but not under the Constitution

    D.   The federal government was divided into three distinct branches under the Articles but not under the Constitution

5.   Which of the following was true under the Articles of Confederation?

    A.   Each state had one vote in Congress

    B.   Amendments to the Articles could be made only by unanimous vote

    C.   Congress had the authority to print money

    D.   All of the above

6.   The term "checks and balances" refers to

    A.   The system of weights and measures created under the Articles of Confederation

    B.   The fact that the Constitution gave each branch of government distinct powers

    C.   The fact that the Constitution gave each branch of government certain powers over the actions of the other branches

    D.   The balance of power between the federal government and the individual states as expressed in the Tenth Amendment

7. The New Jersey Plan presented at the Constitutional Convention of 1787 proposed that

   A. Congress should be divided into two chambers, in which the number of representatives in both should be apportioned according to population
   B. Congress should be divided into two chambers, in which the number of representatives in one chamber should be apportioned according to population while all states should have equal representation in the other chamber
   C. Congress should have only one chamber, in which the number of representatives should be apportioned according to population
   D. Congress should have only one chamber, in which all states should have equal representation

8. The Great Compromise refers to the agreement between

   A. Slave states in the South and free states in the North to admit Missouri as a slave state and Maine as a free state
   B. Small states and large states at the Constitutional Convention to create a bicameral Congress that would preserve the balance of power among the states
   C. Federalists and Anti-Federalists to ratify the Constitution on the condition that the first Congress draft a Bill of Rights
   D. Federalists and Anti-Federalists to designate Washington, D.C., as the new national capital in exchange for debt relief to impoverished farmers

9. Under the Constitution, the president of the United States has the authority to do which of the following?

   A. Declare war
   B. Levy taxes
   C. Veto legislation
   D. All of the above

10.   All of the following are true about the framers of the
      Constitution *except*

      A.   They were all wealthy
      B.   Most of them had *not* been zealous leaders in the
           Revolutionary War
      C.   All were experienced statesmen
      D.   All believed that the Constitution they created was too
           weak

11.   Many Anti-Federalists refused to ratify the Constitution
      unless

      A.   Alexander Hamilton conceded that agriculture was
           more important than manufacturing
      B.   The United States promised to uphold the Franco-
           American alliance of 1778
      C.   A Bill of Rights was added to the Constitution
      D.   George Washington would be the first president of the
           United States

12.   Alexander Hamilton, James Madison, and John Jay wrote
      the Federalist Papers to convince

      A.   Anti-Federalist New Yorkers to ratify the Constitution
      B.   Congress to create a stronger Supreme Court
      C.   Delegates at the Constitutional Convention to
           incorporate a system of checks and balances within the
           Constitution
      D.   Western Pennsylvanians not to participate in the
           Whiskey Rebellion

13.   What does the Tenth Amendment state?

      A.   That Americans have the right to bear arms
      B.   That Americans have the right to free speech, press,
           assembly, and petition
      C.   That those powers not granted to federal government
           are reserved for the states
      D.   That Americans have additional rights beyond those
           enumerated in the Constitution

14. What did the Judiciary Act of 1789 do?

    A. Granted the Supreme Court the power of judicial
       review
    B. Created the federal court system
    C. Limited the powers of the Supreme Court over
       Congress
    D. Declared Adams's "midnight judges" unconstitutional

15. Hamilton's fiscal policy for the United States included all of
    the following *except*

    A. Creating a Bank of the United States
    B. Having Congress assume all national and state debts
       incurred during the Revolutionary War
    C. Encouraging the development of agriculture over
       manufacturing
    D. Levying an excise tax

16. What did the loose constructionists believe?

    A. That the Constitution forbade all governmental actions
       that it did not expressly permit
    B. That the Constitution permitted all governmental
       actions that it did not expressly forbid
    C. That the United States should be a loose confederation
       of states
    D. That the Articles of Confederation should be
       interpreted loosely to allow for the ratification of the
       new Constitution

17. Jeffersonians generally believed that

    A. The Constitution should be interpreted strictly
    B. The United States should uphold the Franco-American
       alliance of 1778
    C. Agriculture should be fostered and protected
    D. All of the above

18. Why did Alexander Hamilton propose the excise tax in 1790?

   A. He wanted the revenue in order to pay off the national and state debts
   B. He disliked western farmers' reliance on whiskey
   C. He wanted to punish Pennsylvanian farmers for the Whiskey Rebellion
   D. He planned to use the revenue to create the Bank of the United States

19. Hamiltonian Federalists hoped that the United States would make a firm alliance with

   A. France
   B. Britain
   C. Spain
   D. Canada

20. The Federalist and Democratic-Republican political parties were born out of

   A. Disagreements at the Constitutional Convention of 1787
   B. A disagreement among the states as to who should be the first president
   C. The debates over ratification of the Constitution
   D. Ideological differences within George Washington's cabinet

21. Western farmers, such as those who revolted in the Whiskey Rebellion, were angry because

   A. Spain had denied Americans access to the Mississippi River
   B. British troops were still stationed in the American Ohio Valley
   C. Native Americans were harassing white settlements
   D. All of the above

22. Why was French Citizen Edmond Genêt rejected as ambassador to the United States in 1793?

    A. He refused to comply with the Neutrality Proclamation

    B. He threatened American shipping interests

    C. All foreigners were deported according to the terms of the Alien Act

    D. He violated the Sedition Act by speaking out against the government

23. What did delegates at the Hartford Convention petition against?

    A. The War of 1812

    B. The ratification of the Constitution

    C. The Alien and Sedition Acts

    D. The Battle of Tippecanoe

24. From what did the delegates at the Hartford Convention draw inspiration for their petition?

    A. The Albany Congress

    B. The Constitutional Convention

    C. The Virginia and Kentucky Resolutions

    D. The Stamp Act Congress

25. All of the following helped cause the War of 1812 *except*

    A. The impressments of American sailors onto British warships

    B. Royal Navy seizures of American merchant ships and cargos

    C. Britain's refusal to remove troops from the Louisiana Territory

    D. Citizen Genêt's efforts to spread anti-British propaganda in order to bring the U.S. into the France's war against Britain

26. How was the Non-Intercourse Act different from the Embargo Act?

   A. The Embargo Act forbade American merchants from trade with all foreign countries; the Non-Intercourse Act banned trade only with Britain and France

   B. The Non-Intercourse Act forbade trade with all foreign nations; the Embargo Act banned trade only with Britain and France

   C. The Embargo Act banned trade with Britain and France; the Non-Intercourse Act promised to restore trade relations with the first country that agreed to respect American neutrality

   D. The Embargo Act banned trade with Britain; the Non-Intercourse Act banned trade with France

27. Why did Congress pass Macon's Bill No. 2 in 1810?

   A. The Embargo and Non-Intercourse Acts had not been effective

   B. American shippers were still illegally trading with foreign countries

   C. Congress was desperate to stimulate the economy

   D. Anti-French sentiment was growing among the American populace

28. The War Hawks in Congress came primarily from

   A. New England
   B. The West and South
   C. The Mid-Atlantic and Northeast
   D. New York

29. The American victory at the 1811 Battle of Tippecanoe

   A. Forced the British to withdraw from the Louisiana Territory

   B. Ended organized Native American resistance to white settlement in the Mississippi basin

   C. Convinced the French to abandon their dreams of retaking Québec

   D. Encouraged Spain to cede Florida to the United States

30. What was the Northwest Confederacy?

    A. The name Congress gave to the territories governed by the Northwest Ordinance of 1787

    B. The collection of states represented at the Hartford Convention

    C. A pan–Native-American alliance west of the Mississippi River

    D. A nickname for the 1810 Congress dominated by War Hawks

31. The 1814 Treaty of Ghent gave Americans all of the following *except*

    A. A new sense of national pride

    B. Clearly defined eastern borders with Canada

    C. British guarantees to respect American shipping rights as a neutral country

    D. British promises to withdraw troops stationed in American territory

32. What did the 1803 Supreme Court decision *Marbury v. Madison* do?

    A. Reaffirmed the Court's power of judicial review

    B. Reaffirmed the Court's supremacy over state courts

    C. Found the Alien and Sedition Acts were unconstitutional

    D. Reaffirmed the Court's right to hear appeals cases

33. In the early 1800s, most Americans were

    A. Merchants

    B. Farmers

    C. Indentured servants

    D. Plantation owners

34. Why did Napoleon sell the Louisiana Territory to the United States?

    A. He didn't want to open another theater in the war against Britain and Spain

    B. He was having trouble controlling the Native Americans in the region

    C. He didn't want the U.S. to become allies with Britain

    D. He needed the money

35. What did Thomas Jefferson's 1808 Embargo Act do?

    A. Forced Britain to declare war on the United States

    B. Prompted France to revoke the Franco-American alliance of 1778

    C. Caused a severe depression in the United States

    D. All of the above

36. The election of 1800 is often referred to as the Revolution of 1800 because

    A. The Democratic-Republicans came to power without any bloodshed

    B. The Federalist Northeast almost seceded from the Union

    C. The Constitution replaced the Articles of Confederation

    D. Daniel Shays marched to Washington, D.C., with 1,500 men to contest the outcome of the election

37. All of the following actions by Thomas Jefferson were in accordance with his interpretation of the Constitution *except*

    A. Authorizing the Louisiana Purchase

    B. Eliminating the national debt

    C. Downsizing of the federal government

    D. Granting more power to the state governments

38. The *Chesapeake* Affair aroused American anger toward

    A. The illegal impressment of American sailors
    B. French attempts to persuade Congress to declare war on Britain in defiance of the Neutrality Proclamation
    C. The Northwest Confederacy west of the Mississippi
    D. New England delegates at the Hartford Convention

39. Jefferson encouraged Congress to pass the Embargo Act in 1808 to punish Britain and France for

    A. Allowing American ships to sail to their countries
    B. Trying to convince the United States to enter the war in Europe
    C. Refusing to recognize U.S. rights as a neutral nation on the high seas
    D. Demanding enormous bribes

40. The Virginia and Kentucky Resolutions stipulated that

    A. States could nullify acts of Congress that they deemed unconstitutional
    B. Women should be granted the right to vote
    C. The War of 1812 was unconstitutional and a purely sectional conflict
    D. The states desired to secede from the Union

41. Jay's Treaty of 1794 stipulated that

    A. Britain would withdraw troops from the Ohio Valley
    B. The United States would pay outstanding debts owed to British merchants
    C. American shippers would receive compensation for illegal seizures
    D. All of the above

42. The motto "Millions for defense, but not one cent for tribute" arose as a response to which event?

    A. The XYZ Affair
    B. The passage of the Alien Act
    C. Illegal British seizures of American merchant ships
    D. The Battle of Tippecanoe

43. What effect did the Alien and Sedition Acts have?

    A.   Ruined the Democratic-Republican Party
    B.   Ruined the Federalist Party
    C.   Helped unify the Democratic-Republican Party
    D.   Helped unify the Anti-Federalist Party

44. The three-fifths clause of the Constitution stated that

    A.   All constitutional amendments had to be approved by three-fifths of the states
    B.   All new laws had to be approved by three-fifths majority vote in Congress
    C.   Each slave counted as three-fifths of a free person for census purposes
    D.   Each Native American counted as three-fifths of a white person for census purposes

45. The authors of the Federalist Papers argued against which widespread belief?

    A.   That republican governments in general were impractical and unrealistic
    B.   That only small countries could successfully be republican
    C.   That slavery is antithetical to republicanism
    D.   That the United States would eventually collapse because it was too divided

46. Federalists cited the elastic clause to justify

    A.   The Bank of the United States
    B.   Assuming all state and federal debts
    C.   Creating the cabinet
    D.   The Alien and Sedition Acts

47. What act did the Northwest Confederacy's leaders believe that the U.S. government had violated?

    A.   The Dawes Severalty Act
    B.   The Indian Intercourse Acts
    C.   The Indian Removal Act
    D.   The Sedition Act

48. Federalists passed the Alien Act in 1798 out of fear that

    A. Democratic-Republicans would contest Adams's election

    B. War Hawks would declare war on Britain

    C. Too many indentured servants from Britain would take American jobs

    D. French immigrants would cause trouble in the United States in the event of a war with France

49. Why did Federalists pass the Sedition Act in 1798?

    A. To weaken or destroy the Democratic-Republican Party

    B. To prevent French revolutionaries from inciting rebellion in the United States

    C. To stifle opposition voiced in the Virginia and Kentucky Resolutions

    D. To punish the French for their impudence in the XYZ Affair

50. The first president of the United States was

    A. George Washington

    B. Alexander Hamilton

    C. John Adams

    D. Benjamin Franklin

ANSWER KEY

1. B; 2. C; 3. A; 4. B; 5. D; 6. C; 7. D; 8. B; 9. C; 10. D; 11. C; 12. A; 13. C; 14. B; 15. C; 16. B; 17. D; 18. A; 19. B; 20. D; 21. D; 22. A; 23. A; 24. C; 25. D; 26. A; 27. C; 28. B; 29. B; 30. C; 31. C; 32. A; 33. B; 34. D; 35. C; 36. A; 37. A; 38. A; 39. C; 40. A; 41. D; 42. A; 43. C; 44. C; 45. A; 46. A; 47. B; 48. D; 49. A; 50. A

SUGGESTIONS FOR FURTHER READING

AMAR, AKHIL REED. *The Bill of Rights: Creation and Reconstruction.* New Haven: Yale University Press, 1998.

AMBROSE, STEPHEN E. *Undaunted Courage: Meriwether Lewis, Thomas Jefferson, and the Opening of the American West.* New York: Simon & Schuster, 1996.

BOYDSTON, JEANNE, NICK CULLATHER, JAN ELLEN LEWIS, MICHAEL MCGERR, AND JAMES OAKES. *Making a Nation: The United States and its People.* New Jersey: Prentice Hall, 2002.

CUNNINGHAM, NOBLE E. *Jefferson vs. Hamilton: Confrontations that Shaped a Nation.* Boston: Bedford/St. Martins, 2000.

FARAGHER, JOHN MACK, MARI JO BUHLE, DANIEL CZITROM, AND SUSAN H. ARMITAGE. *Out of Many: A History of the American People, Volume I.* New Jersey: Prentice Hall, 2003.

HAMILTON, ALEXANDER, JAMES MADISON, AND JOHN JAY. *The Federalist Papers.* New York: Signet Classics, 2003.

HICKEY, DONALD. *The War of 1812: A Forgotten Conflict.* Urbana: University of Illinois Press, 1989.

KENNEDY, DAVID M., LIZABETH COHEN, AND THOMAS A. BAILEY. *The American Pageant.* Boston: Houghton Mifflin, 2002.

WEISBERGER, BERNARD A. *America Afire: Jefferson, Adams, and the Revolutionary Election of 1800.* New York: William Morrow, 2000.

REVIEW & RESOURCES

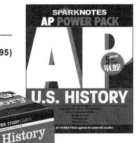